O'Neil Ford Monograph 8
The Little Chapel in the Woods

Denton, Texas, 1938-39

O'Neil Ford & Arch Swank

The O'Neil Ford Monograph Series Volume 8
The Little Chapel in the Woods
O'Neil Ford & Arch Swank

The University of Texas at Austin

O'Neil Ford Chair in Architecture

Editor
Wilfried Wang

Essays
Beth Dodd, Katie Pierce Meyer & Nancy Sparrow;
Brantley Hightower; Kathryn Holliday;
Kathryn O'Rourke; Wilfried Wang

Typography
Victoria Knabe

Copy Editor
Trenton A. Sexton

Dedication
This book is dedicated to the hundreds of volunteers and collaborators who participated in the design and construction of The Little Chapel in the Woods.

Printed and bound in South Korea

Sole Distributor in Europe:
Wasmuth & Zohlen Verlag UG
(haftungsbeschränkt)
Quedlinburger Straße 11
10589 Berlin, Germany
www.wasmuth-verlag.de
info@wasmuth-verlag.de

ISBN 978-3-8030-2214-1

Sole Distributor in the United States of America and Canada
Artbook LLC, D.A.P. / Distributed Art Publishers
75 Broad Street, Suite 630
New York, NY 10004, USA
Tel. (212) 627-1999
www.artbook.com
orders@artbook.com

O'Neil Ford Award for
Design Achievement medallion,
Texas Society of Architects.
Received by Frank Welch, 2015

Perspective of the Resurrection Chapel, Woodland Cemetery, Stockholm, Sigurd Lewerentz, ca.1925

Introduction
Wilfried Wang

Amid the most devastating economic crisis that had ever befallen the USA, there were signs of collective creativity despite tight budgets. In response to the Great Depression, that lasted from the Wall Street Crash of 24 October 1929 to the outbreak of the Second World War, Franklin D. Roosevelt devised a recovery plan, the "New Deal" (1933-1939), that did not merely have an economic effect, but also assured people that individual and collective fates could be guided by thoroughly considered social and political reform programs. The benefits from the New Deal were visible across all scales of the continent, from energy and transport infrastructure to housing, from farms to public art. One small part of this enormous collective effort was the design and construction of The Little Chapel in the Woods (competition in 1938, construction 1939) in Denton, for the Texas State College for Women as it was known then (in 1957 it changed its name to its current version, the Texas Women's University). It was built with the help of the Texas section of the National Youth Administration, and the fieldstone was quarried by members of the Civilian Conservation Corps in Bridgeport, Texas, both part of the New Deal's Works Program Administration (1935-1939, thereafter Works Projects Administration, 1939-1943). Some 300 students of the college were actively involved in the design and construction of parts of the Chapel. It was one of the largest "design-build" projects that students of a college have ever helped to realize.

Exterior view of the Resurrection Chapel, Woodland Cemetery, Stockholm, Sigurd Lewerentz, 1921-1925

The architects of The Little Chapel in the Woods were O'Neil Ford (1905-1982) and Arch B. Swank Jr. (1913-1999 the two collaborated between 1937 and 1941), together with Preston Murdoch Geren Sr. (1891-1969, notably the associate architect to Louis I. Kahn on the Kimbell Art Museum, 1966-1972). Their design clearly expressed their conviction that new buildings should be rooted in the cultural traditions of the context, while also exploring and synthesizing appropriate advances in forms and technology within such transfigured canons, as Brantley Hightower describes in his essay in this monograph. O'Neil Ford, a seasoned traveler of the Texan topography, a keen observer of the Texan flora (as can be gleaned from his sketches of trees and shrubs in this book) and an admirer of all surviving buildings of character, decried the neglect of the natural and built heritage of his beloved state. He admired the fusion of the economy of means with the precise and minimal formal elaboration of quotidian buildings, a love that he expressed in his numerous sketches and etchings, a small selection of which are included in this book; he would enthuse listeners of his

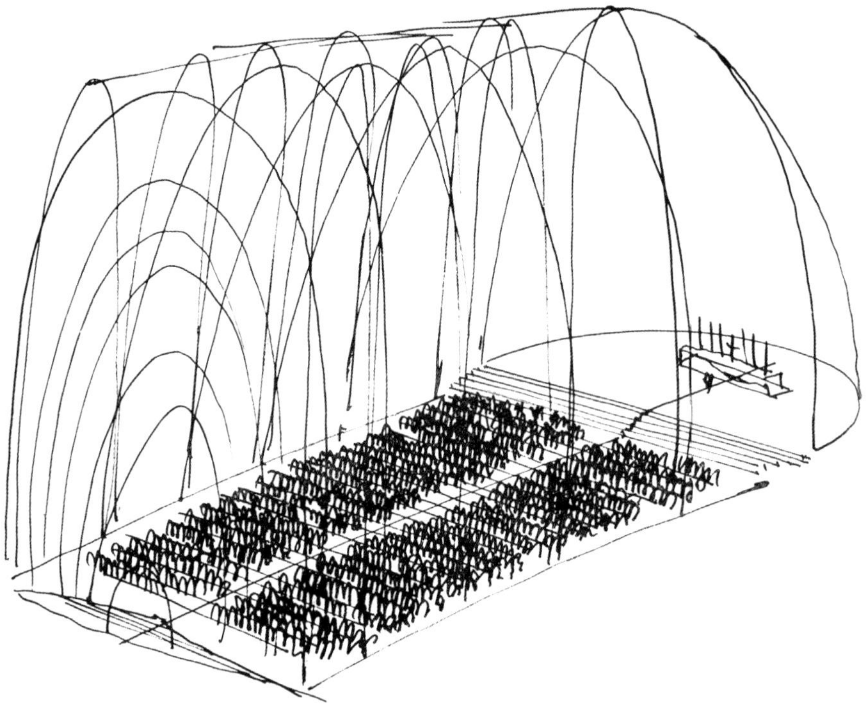

Sketch of the Corpus Christi Church, Aachen, Rudolf Schwarz, 1928-1930

lectures with his pithy and unadorned evocations of Spanish missionary churches or the structural brilliance of *boveda* domes; he gave his audience a piece of his mind when he implored them to respect built history as the incorruptible source of genuine cultural identity. He was no technophile; he saw the threats to cultural cohesion posed by the blind technophilia of his time, yet he was eager to explore new technologies if they advanced architectural quality, as can be seen in his use of the lift-slab method for Trinity University San Antonio (1948 onwards), hyperbolic paraboloid shells for the roofs in the Texas Instruments Semiconductor Building (1956-1958, Dallas), or the bicycle wheel roof for La Villita Assembly Hall (1957-1959, San Antonio). The paraboloid arches in The Little Chapel in the Woods can therefore be seen to foreshadow O'Neil Ford's sustained interest and exploration of structural systems as the scale of his commissions progressed.

The Little Chapel in the Woods is not only a manifesto that lays claim to the power and energy of youth–the product of the National Youth Administration program, and not only an explicit claim to gender equality as expressed in the Chapel's stained glass windows–a topic that Kathryn O'Rourke's essay in this monograph analyzes in depth, but also a concentrated architectural beacon in the flat landscape of north Texas that offers an unwavering shelter in the midst of technological, social, political and cultural change. The churches of the Spanish missions in the Mexican-Texan region served as one of the sources of The Little Chapel in the Woods configurational iconography: a tall hall with a symmetric entrance and a rose window above; on the interior combinations of plastered walls, masonry structural elements and a wooden roof. The Little Chapel in the Woods is an abstracted version of this tradition that deeply engrained in the cultural heritage of this region spanning Mexico and Texas.

However, in the aftermath of the First World War and in the middle of the Great Depression, the Chapel's canonic configuration is not only a religious anchor in the maelstrom, it is the gate that opens the view to messages of change on the interior: in the stained-glass windows and in the concrete filled brick parabolic arches. Notable in the Chapel's design is the simple exterior, on the one hand befitting the scale of the building but also on the other hand a result of a considered response to the process of formal abstraction that underpinned the first wave of modernism. The architects accentuated the Chapel's verticality by means of the dynamism of the parabolic arches (the external cross-sectional dimensions actually measuring 23′ 8″ x 24′ 6″ to the top of the external wall), capped by a roof with an ever so thin edge, a detail that parallels both modernist as well as classicist architects of the time, for example Sigurd

Exterior view of the Corpus Christi Church, Aachen, Rudolf Schwarz, 1928-1930

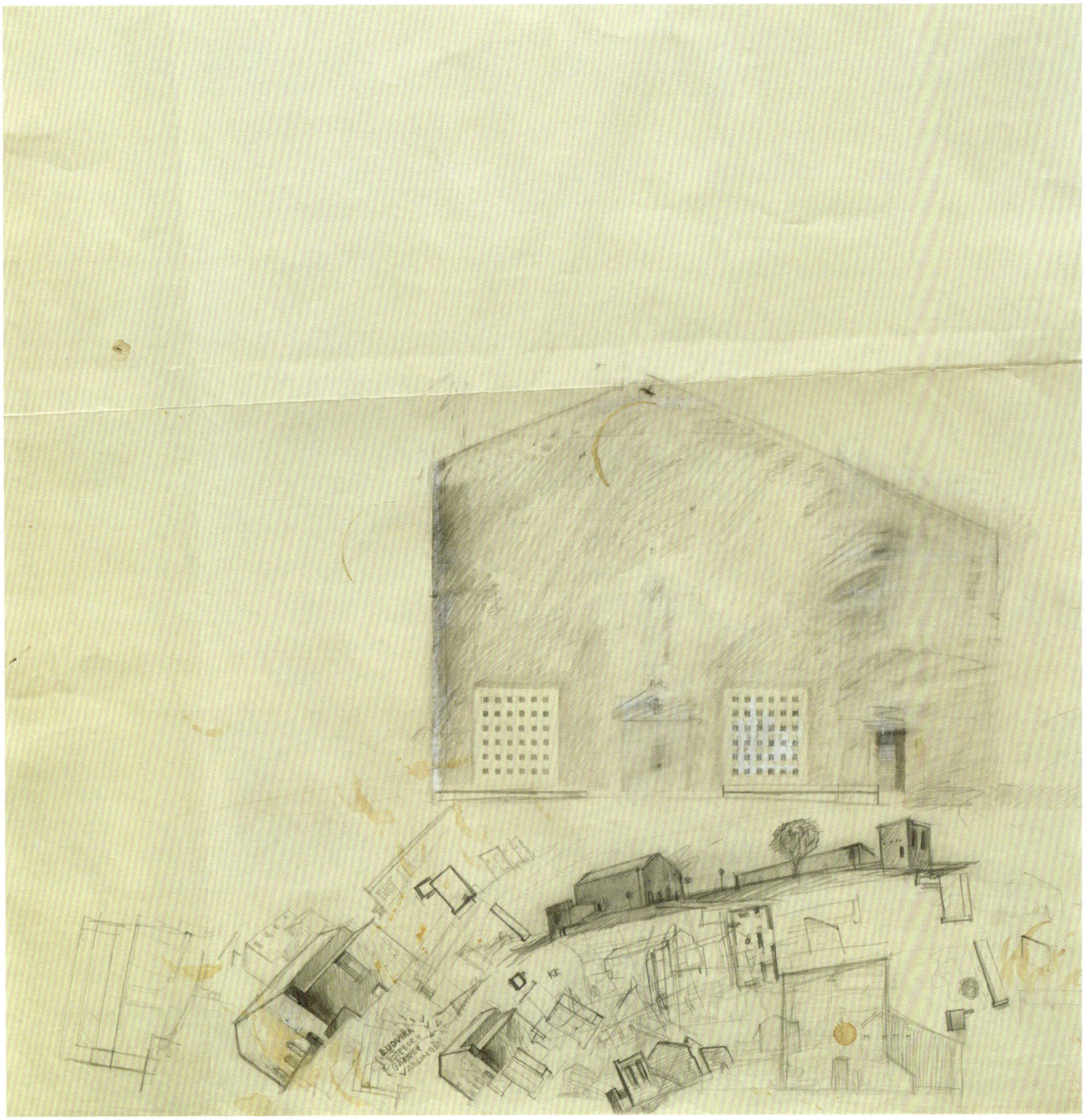

Sketch of Härlanda Church in Gothenburg, Peter Celsing, 1952-1959

Lewerentz' Resurrection Chapel (1921-1925) in Stockholm's Woodland Cemetery and Rudolf Schwarz' Corpus Christi Church in Aachen (1928-1930). The random ashlar fieldstone envelope set itself against the simple form, enlivening the building's mass; the external bases of the paraboloid arches are not simply structural buttresses, they also give the small configuration a sense of stability.

The sequence of parabolic arches, modulated in scale by the last one in front of the chancel, is culminated by the parabolic bay above the altar, like a protective shroud. As if to exaggerate the height of the Chapel, the stained-glass windows were proportioned as narrow vertical bands, framed by plastered walls, that, by virtue of their non-constructive character, allow the brick parabolic arches to be foregrounded. The choice of bricks for the arches, rather than reinforced concrete, underlines the architects' interest in expressing craftsmanship in general, and the effort of the many youths in particular. As with the great brick Gothic cathedrals of northern Europe, the use of a common material such as brick underscored both the constructive daring as well as the collective effort. Furthermore, the ubiquitous knowledge of bricklaying engages observers of such brick structures in a virtual manner in the arches' process of construction, underlining the credibility of the resultant architecture. At a more detailed, personal scale of encounter, users of the Chapel would notice the special care given to the interlaced floor tiling, the carvings of the woodwork such as the pews or the lectern, the purpose made metal work for the main doors, and the spherical lamps.

The combination of design considerations, from the siting in the landscape–see Kathryn Holliday's in depth exploration of this topic in this monograph–to its massing, the eaves of the roof, the fieldstone exterior, the brick arches, the stained-glass windows and the door handles, result in a building that spans from an archaic Christianity to a subtly contemporaneous reinterpretation of religious loftiness. Youths from the National Youth Administration program and from the women's college, under the guidance of architects and teachers, realized this Chapel with a degree of precision and care that stands comparison with the best buildings of the period.

In its synthesis of an archaic configuration with a contemporaneous structural system, The Little Chapel in the Woods embraced similar canonic norms that other chapels of the twentieth century sought in an abstracted manner with their respective innovations. For example, Sigurd Lewerentz' Resurrection Chapel is an exercise in siting an archaic nave in an innovative manner asymmetrically and perpendicularly to the long axial promenade through the woodland cemetery so that the congregation would enter one door and exit another in a symbolic gesture of the circularity of life, or of life's continuity as opposed to the conventional funeral procession with cremation as an endpoint. Lewerentz' adherence to the language of neoclassical architecture provides the necessary stability in contrast to the innovation in the funeral ritual. Rudolf Schwarz' monumental Catholic Corpus Christi Church, in fact supposedly only a parish church, emphasizes the vertical recalling the grandeur of cathedrals, a spatial gesture that is paradoxically amplified

Härlanda Church in Gothenburg, Peter Celsing, 1952-1959

by the dematerialized construction and the minimized number of openings. Both Lewerentz and Schwarz' early churches eschew the display of their real construction, preferring instead to cover the supporting material with plaster and paint, an approach that is reversed in their later buildings.

In 1938, in the same year as O'Neil Ford and Arch Swank use the parabolic arches in their chapel design, Rudolf Schwarz sketches a large church with parabolic arches. Schwarz' design remains on paper, a few months later, the Second World War breaks out; Schwarz never returned to this evocative structural creation reminiscent of the organic loftiness of Gothic cathedrals, however, Ford has another opportunity to include parabolic arches in the Margarite B. Parker Chapel at Trinity University in San Antonio (1966); on this occasion on a truly grand scale.

While The Little Chapel in the Woods is also of a composite structural and constructional nature, on the exterior the architects chose to emphasize the unity of the institution by having the fieldstone

Dimitrios Pikionis, View from the peripteral pergola to Agios Dimitri Loumbardiadis to the Acropolis, Athen 1954–1958

walls wrap the entire configuration. On the interior, the floor and the walls, the arches and the roof are each articulated according to their tectonic role. The Little Chapel in the Woods engages the users with its colors, materiality and crafted details, and thus stands apart from both the abstract classicism as well as the abstract modernism of the two cited cases. Nevertheless, The Little Chapel in the Woods shares the predecessors' preference for the radical normality of the church's configurational typology as a symmetric hall with a saddle roof.

In terms of the crafts articulation, the visibility of constructional details and the continuity in the use of decorative elements, The Little Chapel in the Woods precedes the same interests as are displayed in Dimitri Pikionis' amplification of Agios Dimitris Loumbardiardis Church in Athens (1951-1957) and Peter Celsing's new Härlanda Church in Gothenburg, Sweden (1952-1959). In all three cases one can recognize the assertion in the primacy of skilled labor as the foundation of the built version of culture and as the primary means of bringing an architecture to life.

While early in his career, Pikionis had been an accomplished modernist, in his later phase he turned to an archaeological reinterpretation of primal Greek tectonics as the material-constructive approach to an ontological architecture, that is to say, an architecture that speaks of its own being through the conscious display of its creation: material, constructional detail and composition. Modernist architecture was primarily concerned with the abstraction of form down to its construction. Where materials were displayed, such as the marbles or wood veneers that Adolf Loos or Ludwig Mies van der Rohe were using, they were treated like wall paper. O'Neil Ford, Dimitri Pikionis and Sigurd Lewerentz in their late works, rejected this modernist dematerialization.

Moreover, O'Neil Ford was concerned with place-making. The Little Chapel in the Woods marks the beginning of this concern in a combination of a building and a small architectural landscape. Within this landscape design, The Little Chapel in the Woods sought to offer a bucolic precinct, a moment of shaded respite from the Texan heat under the extensive canopy of the surrounding trees, marked on the ground by low fieldstone retaining walls. O'Neil Ford's involvement in the urban conservation of San Antonio's La Villita began in the last month of works on the Chapel, a project that was to become one of the two main impulses for the resuscitation of downtown San Antonio with its now well-known river-walk.

In a different way, Celsing's Härlanda Church with its linear parish offices and the independently placed belfry harks back to an idea of a religious precinct, unified by the same solid brick construction, embracing in material terms the congregations that gather informally on the exterior before and after services. Further, the notion of communal propinquity is afforded by Pikionis' picturesque assembly of a variety of pergolae, defining a framed precinct without so many words. Pikionis' careful and symbolic augmentation of the 12th century chapel's exterior wall, his addition of fragile and minimal wood structures that casual observers might easily mistake as make-shift assemblage, and the picturesque pavement patterns that show Pikionis as a modern artist who uses stone in place of paint. Similarly, while Ford and Celsing's later buildings appeared to be more in line with technological advancements, both continued to include textures, skilled crafts and traditional decorative elements, none of which strict modernists would ever allow to be associated with.

Eight decades after the completion of The Little Chapel in the Woods, our comprehension of built reality has changed from that of the pre-modernist period. We no longer expect real masonry when we see brick- or stonework. When we enter a new building with arches, we cannot be sure that these are structural; they could be made of plasterboard as decorative elements to elicit a mood. Though modern technology and modern construction may have moved on from the interests that architects such as O'Neil Ford and the others cited in this introduction shared, most contemporary observers of buildings naïvely believe in the reality that they see. Or that they would like to see and believe in. Perhaps this is one reason why The Little Chapel in the Woods enjoys the unbroken admiration of couples who seek a genuine place in which their wedding is celebrated; that their vows be spoken in a substantive and trustworthy place so that they might endure in the same way as The Little Chapel in the Woods.

1 The construction drawings by the office of Preston M. Geren for the Kimball Museum can be found in the Alexander Architectural Archives. A selection of these were published in the special issue of *a+u*, no. 7, 2015.
2 Speck, Larry, "Texas instruments Semiconductor Building", https://larryspeck.com/writing/texas-instruments-semiconductor-building/
3 G.W. Mitchel Contractors, http://gwmitchell.com/la-villita-assembly-building-over-50-years-of-celebrating-san-antonio/
4 Wang, Wilfried, "Architecture as an Extension of Life", *Architect Sigurd Lewerentz*, vol. 1, ed. Claes Dymling, Byggförlaget, Stockholm 1997, 17-21.
5 Wang, Wilfried, *The Architecture of Peter Celsing*, Arkitekturförlaget, Stockholm 1996, 28-33.
6 Dillon, David, *The Architecture of O'Neil Ford: Celebrating Place*, The University of Texas Press, Austin 1999, 47-54.

O'Neil Ford
1948

Contact sheet showing portraits of O'Neil Ford, 1948

Never one place…
Tracing sources and archival documents on The Little Chapel in the Woods

Beth Dodd, Katie Pierce Meyer, Nancy Sparrow

Introduction

The phrase *never one place…*perfectly illustrates the process and challenges of archival research. Research often begins with publications and moves on to primary sources located in archives and personal collections. Each new finding furthers investigation. Examining modern architecture, design and construction, through the interpretation of a single building such as The Little Chapel in the Woods, affords many interesting opportunities to establish context and identify relationships. Connections are made in order to understand the chronology, the people, and the negotiated process of realization. Conducting this type of research is necessary for studying buildings and writing about the built environment, as well as curating exhibitions at the Alexander Architectural Archives.

Research Hub

Never one place, never one collection is a common mantra at the Alexander. The complexity of architectural research is just as challenging as the profession and its creatives, technicians, and clients. The product of their activities and interests are what a scholar might find in architectural repositories around the world. As part of a flagship research university, the resources found within the architectural collections at The University of Texas Libraries are notedly distinctive. Nestled in historic Battle Hall, one has access to monographs and journals, special collections of rare and contextually significant published materials, and an archival repository focusing on Texas architects and buildings. Collecting on a regional scale provides incredible depth of resources. By natural affiliation with the School of Architecture, our collections also support and reflect the teaching and learning needs of future planners, landscape architects, historic preservationists, interior designers and urbanists. Architectural pedagogy draws recognition through international scholars and exhibition loans. The research continuum feeds scholarly output and ingests back into our collections. As the profession collaborates and evolves, so do the records offered in the collections.

The O'Neil Ford collection is one of the most significant and extensive archival resources at the Alexander. As a premiere collection, it reflects nearly all aspects of Ford's creative and productive life. Professional and personal records include project files, papers, diaries, architectural drawings in all phases, photographic material, and ephemera. His core archival collection was a generous donation by the Ford family, with subsequent accruals from the firm Ford Powell Carson, his friends and clients. The Ford collection provides evidence of the origins and practice of his dedication to vernacular architecture, handcraft, historic preservation, innovative design, and his tireless advocacy of education, particularly in the arts. At the Architecture & Planning Library one can find numerous publications by and about Ford and his projects, expanding to digital offerings available beyond the walls of Battle Hall. Countless scholars and researchers have benefited from the donation of this extensive collection, producing theses, dissertations, architectural studio projects and publications.

Regional focus at the Alexander results in an assemblage of affiliated records that offer a narrative about the people involved in the conception, construction, and interpretation of a building. Within the Ford collection are many works by others, including partners such as Jerry Rogers. Numerous other archival collections within the Alexander are related to Ford or his designs, including those of Arch Swank, Preston Geren, Richard Colley, David Williams, Dan Heyn, Sam Zisman, Eugene George, the Buildings of Texas archive, and of course Ford Powell Carson, which attests to the reach of Ford's career and influence beyond Texas. That said, there are numerous collections beyond the Alexander that offer reciprocal correspondence, images, records of clients and professional partnerships. Discovery of these resources has become much more attainable with the advent of the web, the ongoing development of innovative platforms, and a focus on sharing information and data. Federated searching across participating archival repositories is now available through targeted research tools such as the Texas Archival Resources Online site which feeds into global coverage in ArchiveGrid, and the Portal to Texas History which feeds into the Digital Public Library of America.

Demonstrating research

In support of teaching and research, the Alexander offers an exhibition series entitled *To Better Know a Building*. Our intent is to expose a wider range of architecture students to the process and value of archival resources that are generally only available, yet encouraged, in the Alexander's reading room. A single building is selected by popular vote, then archivist Nancy Sparrow conducts the curatorial research. The exhibition is intentionally meant to be documentary rather than interpretive, with the display of items found at the Alexander, such as original drawings, specifications, job files, correspondence, and photographic material. These primary sources are supplemented by publications found at, or through interlibrary loan services provided by the Architecture & Planning Library. The exhibition affords ample opportunity for entire studios to spend quality time with the records produced for the selected building. Repeat viewings result in discussion and discourse that evolve during a studio course. Faculty have also reached out to collaborate in further publications and incorporation of the archives in their curriculum.

The Little Chapel in the Woods at Texas Women's University, Denton, Texas, by architects O'Neil Ford and Arch Swank was the overwhelming winner by popular vote for the second installment in the *To Better Know a Building* series. The exhibition was held from February through August 2015 in the Architecture & Planning Library's historic reading room, fittingly located in the University of Texas' first purpose-built library building, a design by architect Cass Gilbert. The exhibition opening celebration included a thought-provoking lecture prepared by Brantley Hightower to provide historical context.

Researching within a premiere collection such as Ford's is intoxicating to say the least, and especially so when the focus is The Little Chapel. Despite the incredible resources at hand, Nancy Sparrow's research expanded beyond

O'Neil Ford

TEXAS STATE COLLEGE FOR WOMEN

DENTON, TEXAS

OFFICE OF THE PRESIDENT

August 30, 1938

Mr. O'Neil Ford
Cedar Springs Road
Dallas, Texas

Dear Mr. Ford:

I received your special delivery letter last night and was glad to hear from you. Please take all of the time you need in order to perfect the plans.

One thing I am very much interested in is to have an estimate of the cost of the building complete except the organ, chimes, and windows. I am especially pleased that you have interested the two contractors to bid on the complete job. As soon as you have this estimate, I will know better how to proceed. So far, we have had no luck in Washington.

I will be glad to hear from you again.

Yours very truly,

L H Hubbard

L. H. Hubbard, President

LHH:RJ

Correspondence from L.H. Hubbard, President, Texas State College for Women, August 30, 1938

TEXAS STATE COLLEGE FOR WOMEN

DENTON, TEXAS

OFFICE OF THE PRESIDENT

November 15, 1938

Mr. O'Neil Ford
Cedar Springs Road
Dallas, Texas

Dear Mr. Ford:

In accordance with the bill submitted for the model of the chapel, you will find enclosed a check for $33.50 to compensate Miss Betty Irwin, Mr. Bill Allen and Mr. Gerald Rogers for their work on the model of the chapel which I authorized.

Yours very truly,

L H Hubbard

L. H. Hubbard, President

LHH:RJ

P.S. When will the plans be ready?

Correspondence from L.H. Hubbard, President, Texas State College for Women, November 15, 1938

TEXAS STATE COLLEGE FOR WOMEN

DENTON, TEXAS

OFFICE OF THE PRESIDENT

May 4, 1939

Mr. Arch Swank
c/o Ford and Swank
2214 Cedar Springs Road
Dallas, Texas

Dear Mr. Swank:

The Chapel Committee would like to have the following inscriptions placed above the doors at the entrance of the Chapel.

Above the outside entrance,

Worship the Lord in the Beauty of Holiness

Above the door leading from the foyer to the main Chapel,

The Lord is in His Holy Temple, Let all the Earth Keep Silence Before Him

I suppose this lettering would be carved into the woodwork above the door.

I will be glad to talk this over the next time either of you is on the campus.

Yours very truly,

L. H. Hubbard, President

LHH:RJ

Correspondence from L.H. Hubbard, President, Texas State College for Women, May 4, 1939

TEXAS STATE COLLEGE FOR WOMEN

DENTON, TEXAS

OFFICE OF THE PRESIDENT

August 25, 1939

Mr. O'Neil Ford
2214 Cedar Springs
Dallas, Texas

Dear Mr. Ford:

In accordance with your recommendation made to me this morning by Mr. Ledlow, I am authorizing your brother to secure such screws and other small items from Cowser & Company that he will need for the chapel furniture. I hope that this work is proceeding to your satisfaction.

In regard to the platform that is to be placed under the altar, I have asked Mr. Hodges not to build it out of concrete. I would like to wait until the altar is completed and in position, and then build this platform out of wood and in keeping with it. In this way we can get a better balance between the two.

Yours very truly,

L. H. Hubbard, President

LHH:JH

Correspondence from L.H. Hubbard, President, Texas State College for Women, August 25, 1939

our local holdings to find answers to common architectural research queries. In the following passage, she demonstrates her explorative process and findings as she prepared for the exhibition.

Curatorial Process

The research agenda for the *To Better Know a Building* series focuses on finding evidence to contextualize the architect, the design and realization of the project, and the relationships established along the way. For The Little Chapel in the Woods, we asked the following questions:

- What do we know about Ford? Is there evidence of his knowledge on vernacular architecture, regionalism, parabolic arches? Are there publications by Ford? What was in his library? Did he write specifically about modernism or The Little Chapel in the Woods?

- How were the relationships developed between the client and architects? Check for job files, diary entries. The client was the head of Texas Women's University. What is in their archives? The National Youth Administration provided support, so check the National Archives.

- Who did Ford collaborate with and influence on this project? Who were the agents and what were their roles? Check the drawings, brochures, diary entries to see what students and faculty were involved.

- What was the process of realizing the project? What was the chronology? Follow the money and diary entries; design sketches to working drawings; period photography from construction to completion.

- Where are the gaps in the collection? Are records available in other archives? Are there human resources?

The research began by retrieving published sources to help create the narrative for the exhibition, thus drawing on writer and architectural historian Mary Carolyn George's *O'Neil Ford, Architect*, 1992 and architecture critic David Dillon's *The Architecture of O'Neil Ford: Celebrating Place*, 1999. George's archival collection is located at The University of Texas at San Antonio. It includes her extensive research interview tapes, transcripts, notes and copies of correspondence, as well as evidence that she consulted the David Williams collection at the Dupré Library, University of Louisiana at Lafayette. David Dillon was an acclaimed architecture critic for the *Dallas Morning News* from 1983 to 2006. His collection contains his professional papers, writing and research materials, correspondence, interviews, and subject files, all located in the Special Collections at The University of Texas at Arlington Library. Leads were also found in published works before diving into the archives. Details of these findings are documented in the following description of the exhibition.

Introduction

The graphics for the exhibit poster introduced The Little Chapel in the Woods by overlaying an architectural drawing onto a historic photograph created by the library's communications officer, Travis Willmann. The introductory text panel explained the purpose of the series and was followed by reprints from the Ford collection of an article from the influential architectural journal, Pencil Points dated February 1940 titled *Chapel in the Woods*. The article lays out the program, design and details for the chapel including the involvement of the college students and the National Youth Administration, a New Deal program, in the realization of the project. It is a testament to the project that First Lady Eleanor Roosevelt attended and presented remarks at the chapel's dedication ceremony.

Biographical Information

Biographies of the two principal architects were reproduced from the Alexander's online finding aids for the O'Neil Ford and Arch Swank collections, providing brief introductions to their lives and work. A contemporaneous portrait of O'Neil Ford, dated 1939, came from the Ford collection. No photograph of Arch Swank could be found in our collections, so permission was sought to reproduce a portrait of Ford and Swank at a drafting table dated 1938 as published in George's monograph courtesy of Wanda Graham Ford.

Architect's own words

The *To Better Know a Building* series is enriched by evidence of the architect's own thoughts on details of the design process. When possible, quotes which illustrate the architect's philosophies concerning architecture were included. Sources were drawn from the archival collection as well as publications, accompanied by design

TEXAS STATE COLLEGE FOR WOMEN

DENTON, TEXAS

OFFICE OF THE PRESIDENT

October 25, 1939

Messrs. Ford and Swank
2214 Cedar Springs Road
Dallas, Texas

Gentlemen:

We would like very much to have you sit on the platform on the occasion of the dedication of the College Chapel, Wednesday, November 1, at 3:45 p.m.

Yours very truly,

L. H. Hubbard

L. H. Hubbard, President

LHH:RJ

Correspondence from L.H. Hubbard, President, Texas State College for Women, October 25, 1939

New Mexico Church, engraving by O'Neil Ford, 1928

drawings, sketches, and photographs providing visual documentation of structural and material ideas.

Another resource that was found to be well suited for this purpose, is located in the Architecture & Planning Library. *Lessons in Looking: dialogues with O'Neil Ford, architect*, was published by the Learning about Learning Educational Foundation in 1981. A publicity brochure in the Ford collection for the publication explains, "*Learning to Look* was a series of dialogues selected from videotapes of San Antonio architect O'Neil Ford and Texas students. In these dialogues, Mr. Ford illustrates his ideas through slides from his extensive collection and through drawings of architectural concepts and buildings yet to be undertaken."

Design Program

The following quote from George's publication describes the program for the chapel, "The president of the Texas State College for Women in Denton, Dr. L.H. Hubbard had long dreamed of a small chapel intended primarily as a "haven for prayer and meditation but which would afford small groups accommodations for religious services. It would be non-sectarian and uniform in its religious appeal."[1] George cites both the 1940 *Pencil Points* article and the chapel's dedication brochure from the Ford collection that was displayed in the exhibit along with the program.

Substantial documentation contained in the O'Neil Ford collection was reviewed to illustrate and enrich the narrative. Ford's collection includes over 27 linear feet of project records which include notes, correspondence, contracts, specifications, reports, vendor/contractor information, photographs, sketches, and folded drawings. In a perfect world, a collection would have all the project correspondence written between the architect and the client, his suppliers and contractors, to portray their relationships during the design and construction of a project. Seldom is it possible to find evidence from both sides of the conversation, leaving only a one-sided affair. In 2005, to the delight of the Alexander Architectural Archives, a donation of thirty-one diaries from the Ford family was accepted, knowing how valuable these diaries would prove to be for researchers. The first diary is from 1939. The diaries and the correspondence are incredibly informative. The correspondence is particularly useful to illuminate the relationship with the client, as Ford's diary captures his interactions with other members of the project team, decisions made with others about materials, and his sense of satisfaction or frustration during the project. Relevant diary entries were displayed alongside correspondence to help create a timeline for the process of realizing the design and construction of the chapel.

Design Inspiration

"The source of Ford's inspiration for The Little Chapel in the Woods is thought to be revealed in his drawing 'New Mexico Church' which was published in *Southwest Review* (Winter 1932)."[2] For the exhibit, a scan of this drawing from the George publication had to be used, placing it next to early design drawings for the chapel. Nancy was delighted to eventually discover the original engraving for the 1928 inspiration sketch in the Ford collection for inclusion in this essay.

References to an essay by Thomas Broad and O'Neil Ford titled Toward a New Architecture, with Ford's portion labeled *Organic Building* in the same *Southwest Review* issue appeared in both publications by George and Dillon. It was not possible to locate a copy of the journal in either the Ford collection or the University of Texas Libraries, so a copy was secured through the Interlibrary Loan Get a Scan Service. This early publication reveals many of Ford's thoughts about architecture and modernism and explicitly mentions Eugène Freyssinet's Orly airplane hangar as structural inspiration. "Again, there are few examples of the use of that perfect symbol of structure the line that has its ends in infinity, a static, moving, and beautiful curve–the parabola. The great airplane hangar at Orly, near Paris, is a superb work, a parabolic vault 1,000 feet long and 385 feet wide, built of a concrete shell varying from 8 to 3 1/2 inches in thickness and having no beams or girders."[3] This quote was paired with a photograph of the Orly airplane hangar placed next to the two drawings for the nave arch and the chancel arch.

Design Process

Early design drawings for the chapel from the Ford collection, an engraving of a Ford sketch, and a quote from George's publication document the design process. As mentioned above, gathering insights and quotes from publications informed the narrative for the exhibit. Interspersed throughout the exhibit were all of the original pencil on trace construction drawings that included foundations, floor plans, elevations, cross sections, arch drawings and details. Project and construction photographs from the collection as well as from

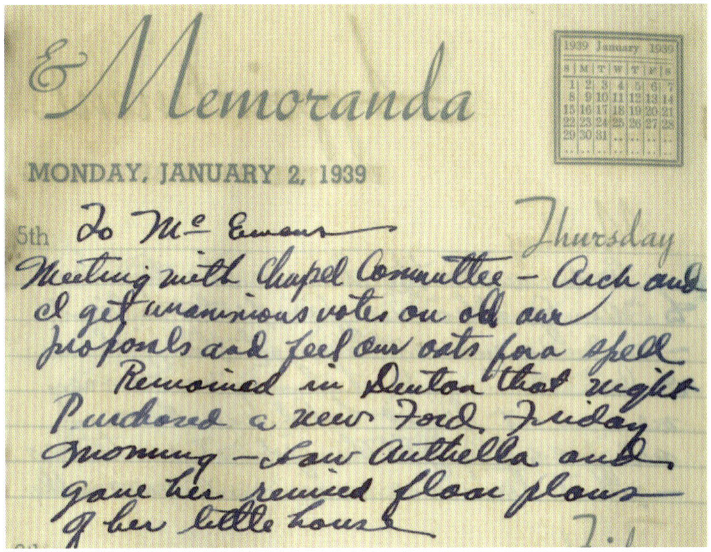
& Memoranda

MONDAY, JANUARY 2, 1939

5th Thursday

To McEwans—
Meeting with Chapel Committee – Arch and I get unanimous votes on all our proposals and feel our oats for a spell
Remained in Denton that night
Purchased a new Ford Friday morning – Saw Authella and gave her revised floor plans of her little house

"Meeting with Chapel Committee - Arch and I get unanimous vote on all our proposals and feel our oats for a spell…" - Ford diary entry, January 5, 1939.

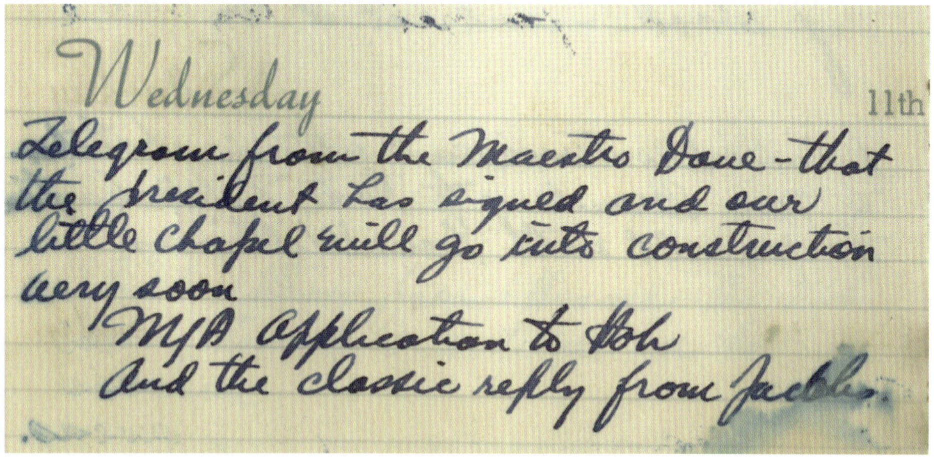
Wednesday 11th

Telegram from the Maestro Dave – that the president has signed and our little chapel will go into construction very soon
NYA Application to [illegible]
And the classic reply from Jacobs.

"Telegram from the Maestro Dave (David Williams) – that the president has signed and our little chapel will go into construction very soon… NYA (National Youth Administration) Application to (unclear) and the classic reply from Jacobs." Ford Diary entry, January 11, 1939

O'NFM_8

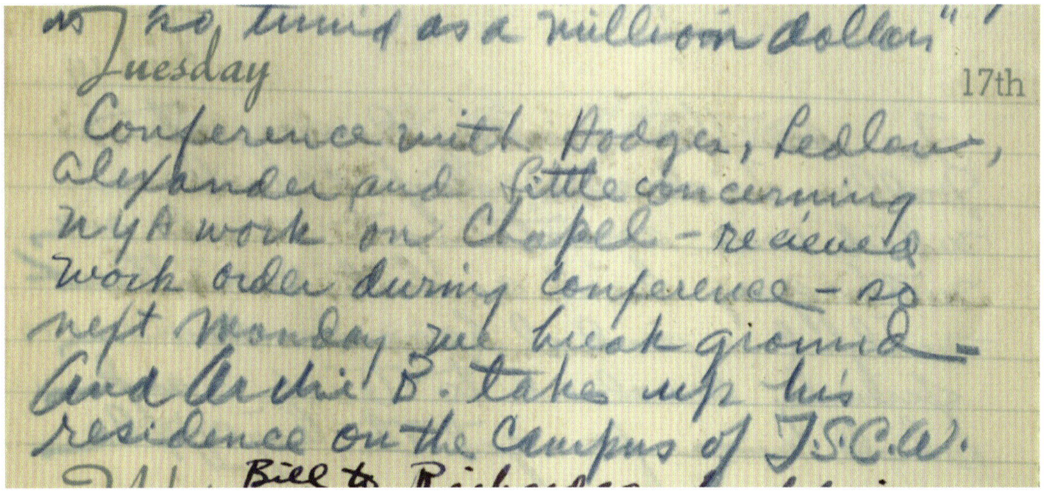
Tuesday 17th

Conference with Hodges, Ledlow, Alexander and Little concerning NYA work on Chapel – received work order during conference – so next Monday we break ground – And Archie B. takes up his residence on the Campus of T.S.C.W.

"Conference with Hodges, Ledlow, Alexander and Little concerning NYA (National Youth Administration) work on Chapel - received work order during conference - so next Monday we break ground - and Arch B." Ford Diary entry, January 17, 1939

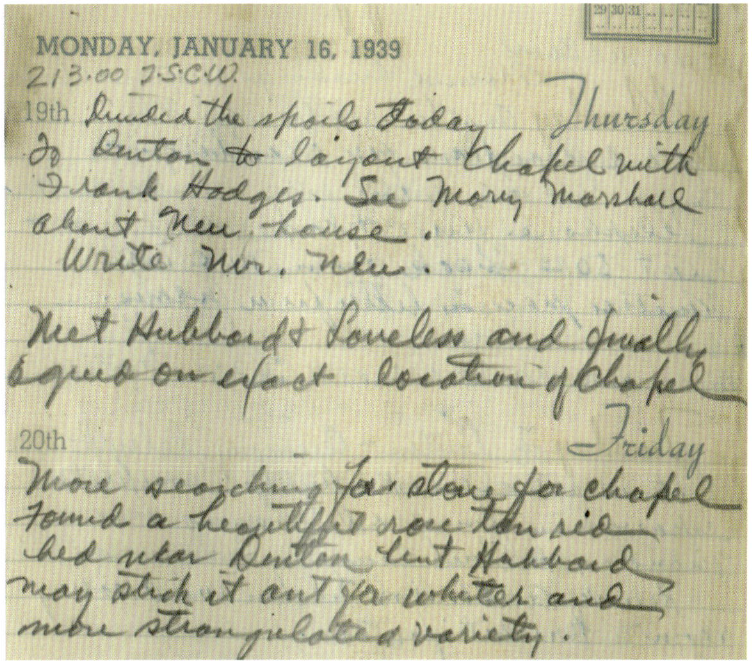

"Divided the spoils today - To Denton to layout the chapel with Frank Hodges...
Meet Hubbard and Loveless and finally agreed on exact location of chapel". Ford diary entry, January 19, 1939

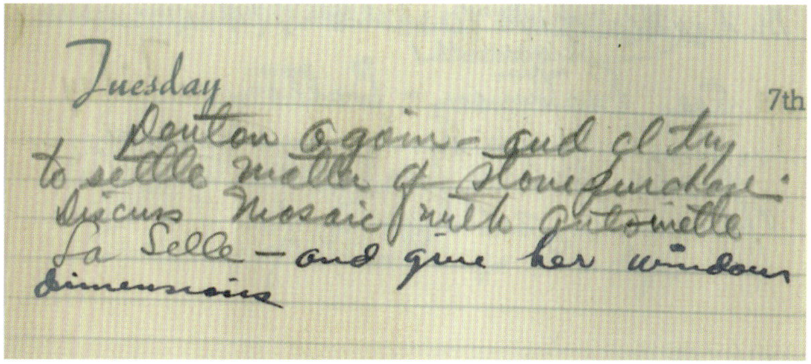

"Denton again - and I try to settle matter of stone purchase. Discuss Mosaic with Antoinette La Selle - and give her window dimensions" Ford diary entry, February 7, 1939

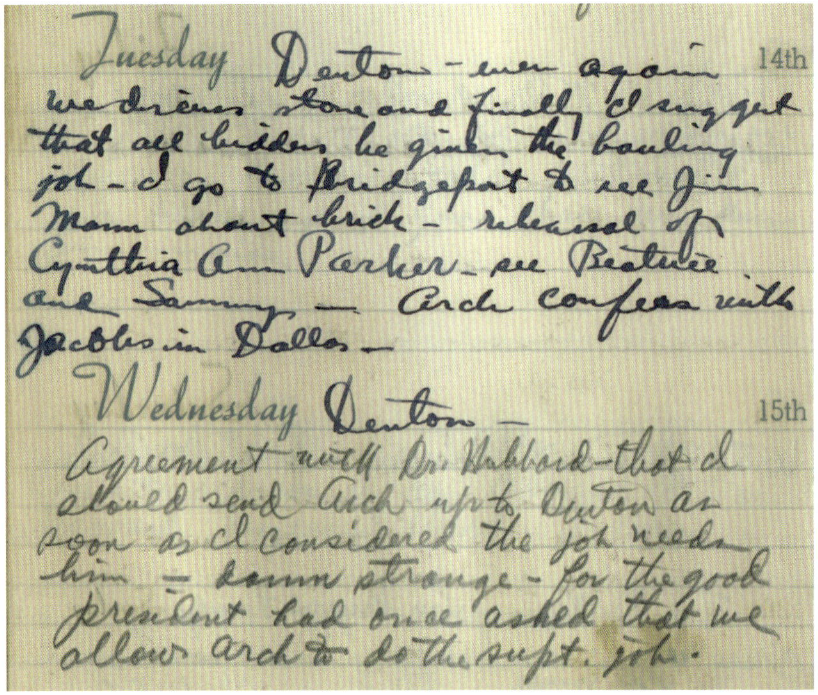

Tuesday Denton - ever again windows stone and finally I suggest that all bidders be given the hauling job - I go to Bridgeport to see Jim Mann about brick - rehearsal of Cynthia Ann Parker - see Beatrice and Sammy - Arch confers with Jacobs in Dallas - 14th

Wednesday Denton - 15th

Agreement with Dr. Hubbard - that I should send Arch up to Denton as soon as I considered the job needed him - damn strange - for the good president had once asked that we allow Arch to do the supt. job.

"Denton - ever again windows, stone and finally I suggest that all bidders be given the hauling job - I go to Bridgeport to see Jim Mann about brick... "

"Denton - Agreement with Dr. Hubbard that I should send Arch up to Denton as soon as I considered the job needed him - damn strange - for the good president had once asked that we allow Arch to do the supt. job." Ford Diary entry February 14-15, 1939

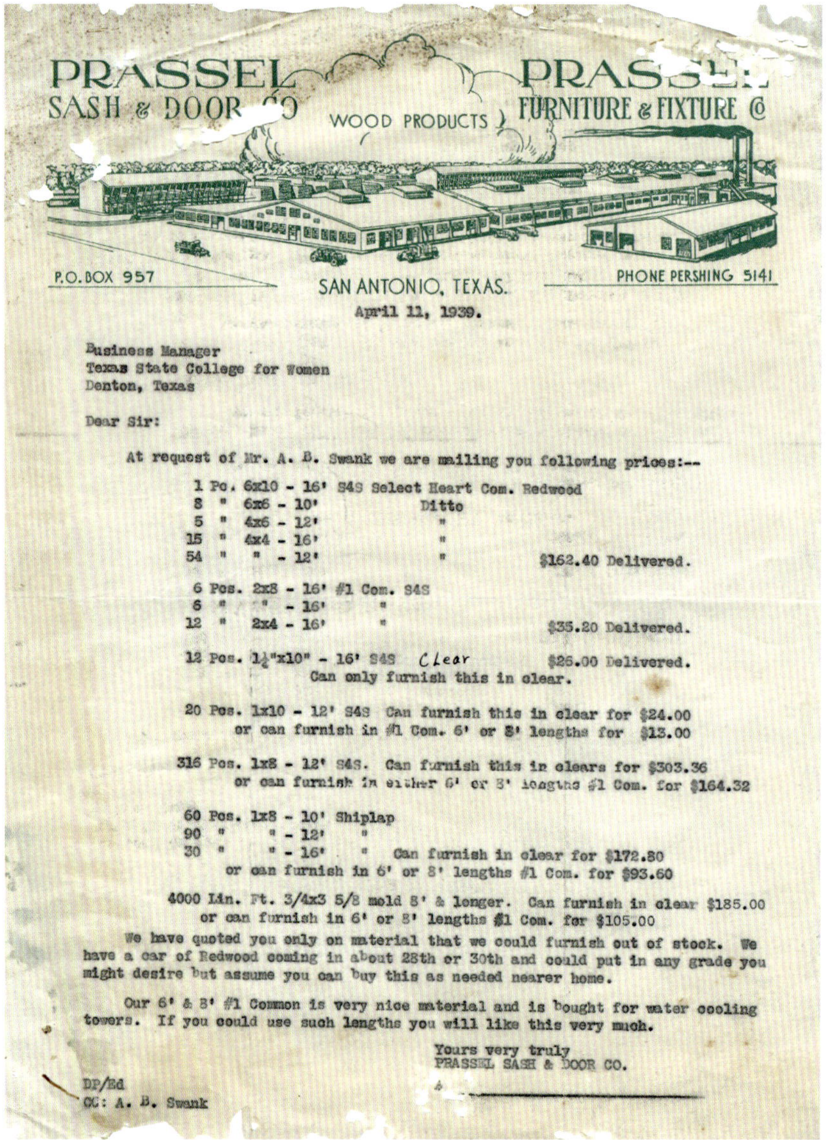

PRASSEL SASH & DOOR CO — WOOD PRODUCTS — PRASSEL FURNITURE & FIXTURE CO

P.O. BOX 957 SAN ANTONIO, TEXAS. PHONE PERSHING 5141

April 11, 1939.

Business Manager
Texas State College for Women
Denton, Texas

Dear Sir:

At request of Mr. A. B. Swank we are mailing you following prices:--

1 Pc. 6x10 - 16' S4S Select Heart Com. Redwood
8 " 6x6 - 10' Ditto
5 " 4x6 - 12' "
15 " 4x4 - 16' "
54 " " - 12' " $162.40 Delivered.

6 Pcs. 2x8 - 16' #1 Com. S4S
6 " " - 16' "
12 " 2x4 - 16' " $35.20 Delivered.

12 Pcs. 1¼"x10" - 16' S4S Clear $26.00 Delivered.
Can only furnish this in clear.

20 Pcs. 1x10 - 12' S4S Can furnish this in clear for $24.00
or can furnish in #1 Com. 6' or 8' lengths for $13.00

316 Pcs. 1x8 - 12' S4S. Can furnish this in clears for $303.36
or can furnish in either 6' or 8' lengths #1 Com. for $164.32

60 Pcs. 1x8 - 10' Shiplap
90 " " - 12' "
30 " " - 16' " Can furnish in clear for $172.80
or can furnish in 6' or 8' lengths #1 Com. for $93.60

4000 Lin. Ft. 3/4x3 5/8 mold 8' & longer. Can furnish in clear $185.00
or can furnish in 6' or 8' lengths #1 Com. for $105.00

We have quoted you only on material that we could furnish out of stock. We have a car of Redwood coming in about 28th or 30th and could put in any grade you might desire but assume you can buy this as needed nearer home.

Our 6' & 8' #1 Common is very nice material and is bought for water cooling towers. If you could use such lengths you will like this very much.

Yours very truly
PRASSEL SASH & DOOR CO.

DP/Ed
CC: A. B. Swank

Cost estimate by Prassel Sash & Door Co., April 11, 1939

O'NFM_8

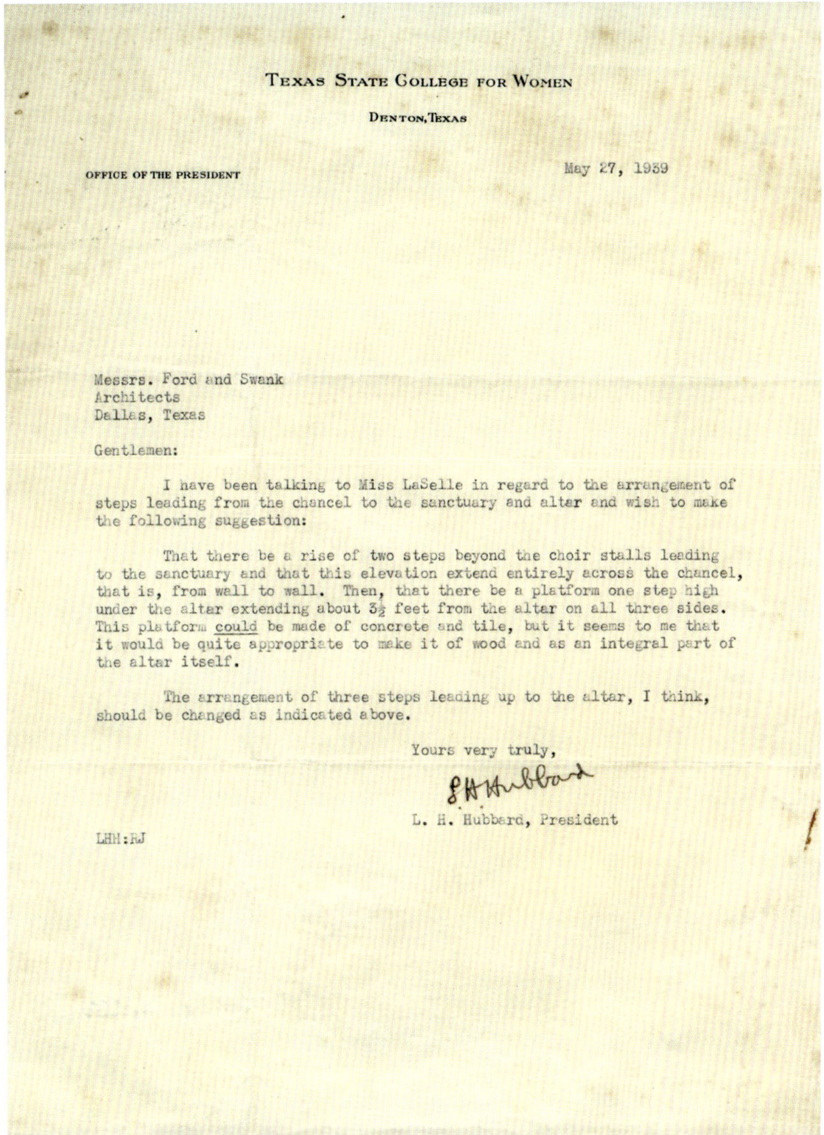

TEXAS STATE COLLEGE FOR WOMEN

DENTON, TEXAS

OFFICE OF THE PRESIDENT

May 27, 1939

Messrs. Ford and Swank
Architects
Dallas, Texas

Gentlemen:

I have been talking to Miss LaSelle in regard to the arrangement of steps leading from the chancel to the sanctuary and altar and wish to make the following suggestion:

That there be a rise of two steps beyond the choir stalls leading to the sanctuary and that this elevation extend entirely across the chancel, that is, from wall to wall. Then, that there be a platform one step high under the altar extending about 3½ feet from the altar on all three sides. This platform could be made of concrete and tile, but it seems to me that it would be quite appropriate to make it of wood and as an integral part of the altar itself.

The arrangement of three steps leading up to the altar, I think, should be changed as indicated above.

Yours very truly,

L. H. Hubbard, President

LHH:RJ

Correspondence from L.H. Hubbard, President, Texas State College for Women, May 27, 1939

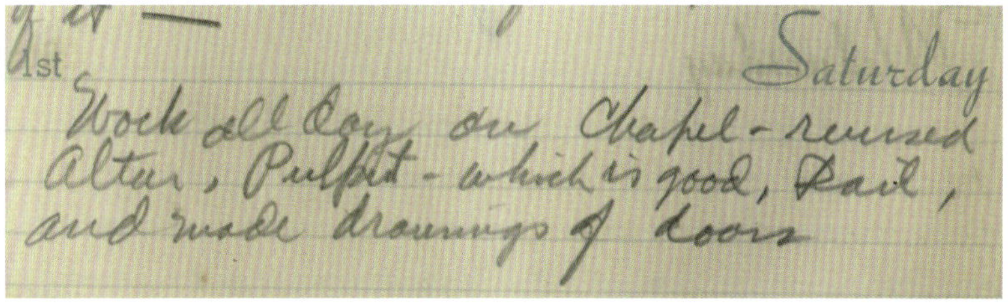

"Work all day on Chapel - revised Altar, Pulpit–which is good, Rail, and made drawings of doors."
Ford Diary entry July 1, 1939

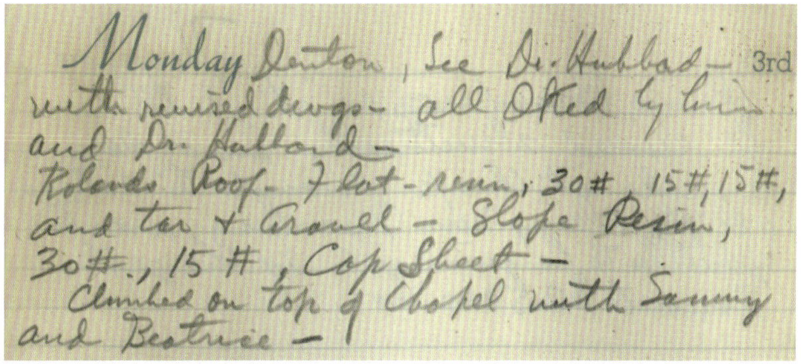

"Denton, See Dr. Hubbard - with revised drawings–all OKed by (unclear) and Dr.Hubbard– Roland's roof … (references work on Roland and Authella Hersh house, Ford's sister and brother-in-law) Climbed on top of Chapel with Sammy and Beatric –" Ford Diary entry July 3, 1939

The Little Chapel-in-the-Woods Texas Woman's University

Welcome to the Little Chapel-in-the-Woods

The peacefulness and beauty of the Little Chapel-in-the-Woods at the Texas Woman's University and the quiet blending of nature and art in this wooded setting have provided thousands of students, families, and friends with rich memories. Enjoy your visit to the Chapel, take time to look at its stained glass windows and to find a moment of quiet meditation, and return often to renew your experience in this very special place.

A long-cherished dream of former TWU President Dr. L.H. Hubbard, the Little Chapel-in-the-Woods was constructed in 1939 from private contributions initiated by the W.R. Nicholson Family of Longview in addition to a grant from the National Youth Administration. Molly Stinson and Elida M. Pearson, co-chairmen of the Student-Faculty Chapel Fund, were tireless in their efforts to raise funds. Designed by the late Dallas architect O'Neil Ford, his partner A.B. Swank of Dallas, and associate Preston M. Geren of Fort Worth, the Chapel was constructed of native gray fieldstone brought from Bridgeport. Dorothy LaSelle, TSCW (Texas State College for Women, as TWU was formerly named) associate professor of art, was designated director of the Chapel Arts Projects. Other members of the Art Department assisting with the project were Marjorie Baltzel, Edith Brisac, Lura Kendrick, Thetis Lemmon, Mary Marshall, Hazel Reneau, and Coreen Spellman. Master artisans supervised the work of some 80 Denton County youth in the stone, brick, and carpentry work; and Miss LaSelle supervised more than 300 students in the design and execution of all of the art work in the Chapel.

Ten stained glass windows, visible from the nave, depict the theme "Woman Ministering to Human Needs." Students began the window designs by sketching live models, and they carried the project through the painting and firing of the glass. The largest and most prominent window, the motherhood window in the chancel, is a triptych (10'x15') dedicated to the ideal woman. Eight slender (2½'x17') windows, four on each side of the nave, are dedicated to women who distinguished themselves and benefited civilization through their professions—nursing, teaching, science, and social service on the west, and speech, literature, dance, and music on the east. The tenth window, an abstract rose window above the entrance, signifies the renewal of faith through communion with nature. The small window in the vestibule is the signature window. In it the builders, donors, and decorators of the Chapel are shown in characteristic pose.

Although the windows have been described as the most outstanding feature of the Chapel, students were equally creative in planning and executing the saw-pierced and riveted brass lighting fixtures, the individually painted beams, and the exquisite wood carvings. Rugs were made to cover the floor of rustic tile. The hand-carved beech pews accommodate approximately 100 people and a small balcony seats about 25. The Chapel houses a two-manual and pedal Allen digital computer organ, given in 1982 by TWU alumna Mabel Scofield Maddox and dedicated in her honor.

Constructed more for private meditation and prayer than for formal services, the Chapel has, nevertheless, become the setting for many student and alumnae weddings. The first marriage took place on September 23, 1939, before an improvised altar in the unfinished Chapel.

The Chapel was still unfinished when Eleanor Roosevelt participated in the dedication ceremonies on November 1, 1939; but work had progressed far enough that the college bulletin of that date could report: "Critics pronounce this one of the nation's outstanding amateur art projects." Conceived as a work of art, the Chapel also was planned to encourage students' spiritual development. The heavy mahogany door was intended to be open at all times to all students.

The following individuals planned, designed, and/or executed the Chapel windows:

Eloise Carriker	*Lura Mae Kendrick*
Mary Ann Chadick	*Dorothy A. LaSelle*
Ivy May Chollar	*Beatrice Paschall*
Mary Cook	*Nora May Pierce*
Helen Crain	*Coreen M. Spellman*
Lucille Cudd	*Betty Winston*
Billie Marie Culwell	*Marilyn Yates*

Advanced History of Art Class, 1939

The Little Chapel-in-the-Woods is maintained through private contributions. If you have questions about the use of the Chapel, or wish to contribute to the Chapel Fund, please contact the Office of Student Life, Texas Woman's University, P.O. Box 22305, Denton, Texas 76204.

The information for this brochure was obtained from the following sources:

Dorothy A. LaSelle, *Iconographies of Stained Glass Windows* (Denton, Texas: Texas State College for Women Press), 1949.

Joyce Thompson, *Marking a Trail: A History of the Texas Woman's University* (Denton, Texas: The Texas Woman's University Press), 1982.

The Little Chapel-in-the-Woods Texas Woman's University

Welcome to the Little Chapel-in-the-Woods

The peacefulness and beauty of the Little Chapel-in-the-Woods at the Texas Woman's University and the quiet blending of nature and art in this wooded setting have provided thousands of students, families, and friends with rich memories. Enjoy your visit to the Chapel, take time to look at its stained glass windows and to find a moment of quiet meditation, and return often to renew your experience in this very special place.

A long-cherished dream of former TWU President Dr. L.H. Hubbard, the Little Chapel-in-the-Woods was constructed in 1939 from private contributions initiated by the W.R. Nicholson Family of Longview in addition to a grant from the National Youth Administration. Molly Stinson and Elida M. Pearson, co-chairmen of the Student-Faculty Chapel Fund, were tireless in their efforts to raise funds. Designed by the late Dallas architect O'Neil Ford, his partner A.B. Swank of Dallas, and associate Preston M. Geren of Fort Worth, the Chapel was constructed of native gray fieldstone brought from Bridgeport. Dorothy LaSelle, TSCW (Texas State College for Women, as TWU was formerly named) associate professor of art, was designated director of the Chapel Arts Projects. Other members of the Art Department assisting with the project were Marjorie Baltzel, Edith Brisac, Lura Kendrick, Thetis Lemmon, Mary Marshall, Hazel Reneau, and Coreen Spellman. Master artisans supervised the work of some 80 Denton County youth in the stone, brick, and carpentry work; and Miss LaSelle supervised more than 300 students in the design and execution of all of the art work in the Chapel.

Ten stained glass windows, visible from the nave, depict the theme "Woman Ministering to Human Needs." Students began the window designs by sketching live models, and they carried the project through the painting and firing of the glass. The largest and most prominent window, the motherhood window in the chancel, is a triptych (10'x15') dedicated to the ideal woman. Eight slender (2½'x17') windows, four on each side of the nave, are dedicated to women who distinguished themselves and benefited civilization through their professions—nursing, teaching, science, and social service on the west, and speech, literature, dance, and music on the east. The tenth window, an abstract rose window above the entrance, signifies the renewal of faith through communion with nature. The small window in the vestibule is the signature window. In it the builders, donors, and decorators of the Chapel are shown in characteristic pose.

Rich in symbolism, the windows feature outstanding women in the professions along with appropriate quotations. Florence Nightingale, Helen Keller and her teacher Anne Sullivan, Isadora Duncan, Ruth St. Denis, Martha Graham, and Doris Humphrey are among the identifiable characters; window inscriptions include quotations from Florence Nightingale, Mary Lyon (founder of Mt. Holyoke), Marie Curie, Jane Addams, George Eliot, and Psalm 149. Included is the chancel window with its three panels symbolizing the good woman and mother, as described in Proverbs 31. The windows tell a story; but more than just relating a history or presenting a roster of well-known names, they symbolize the attitudes and ideals these famous women epitomize. For every iconographical scheme the aim was to interpret the compelling and heartfelt beliefs by which women have benefited the world because they have sustained their faith in life. Their acts are designed into the patterns; their vital words are printed on the glass.

Rich in symbolism, the windows feature outstanding women in the professions along with appropriate quotations. Florence Nightingale, Helen Keller and her teacher Anne Sullivan, Isadora Duncan, Ruth St. Denis, Martha Graham, and Doris Humphrey are among the identifiable characters; window inscriptions include quotations from Florence Nightingale, Mary Lyon (founder of Mt. Holyoke), Marie Curie, Jane Addams, George Eliot, and Psalm 149. Included is the chancel window with its three panels symbolizing the good woman and mother, as described in Proverbs 31. The windows tell a story; but more than just relating a history or presenting a roster of well-known names, they symbolize the attitudes and ideals these famous women epitomize. For every iconographical scheme the aim was to interpret the compelling and heartfelt beliefs by which women have benefited the world because they have sustained their faith in life. Their acts are designed into the patterns; their vital words are printed on the glass.

Although the windows have been described as the most outstanding feature of the Chapel, students were equally creative in planning and executing the saw-pierced and riveted brass lighting fixtures, the individually painted beams, and the exquisite wood carvings. Rugs were made to cover the floor of rustic tile. The hand-carved beech pews accommodate approximately 100 people and a small balcony seats about 25. The Chapel houses a two-manual and pedal Allen digital computer organ, given in 1982 by TWU alumna Mabel Scofield Maddox and dedicated in her honor.

Constructed more for private meditation and prayer than for formal services, the Chapel has, nevertheless, become the setting for many student and alumnae weddings. The first marriage took place on September 23, 1939, before an improvised altar in the unfinished Chapel.

The Chapel was still unfinished when Eleanor Roosevelt participated in the dedication ceremonies on November 1, 1939; but work had progressed far enough that the college bulletin of that date could report: "Critics pronounce this one of the nation's outstanding amateur art projects." Conceived as a work of art, the Chapel also was planned to encourage students' spiritual development. The heavy mahogany door was intended to be open at all times to all students.

The following individuals planned, designed, and/or executed the Chapel windows:

Eloise Carriker
Mary Ann Chadick
Ivy May Chollar
Mary Cook
Helen Crain
Lucille Cudd
Billie Marie Culwell
Lura Mae Kendrick
Dorothy A. LaSelle
Beatrice Paschall
Nora May Pierce
Coreen M. Spellman
Betty Winston
Marilyn Yates

Advanced History of Art Class, 1939

The Little Chapel-in-the-Woods is maintained through private contributions. If you have questions about the use of the Chapel, or wish to contribute to the Chapel Fund, please contact the Office of Student Life, Texas Woman's University, P.O. Box 22305, Denton, Texas 76204.

The information for this brochure was obtained from the following sources:

Dorothy A. LaSelle, *Iconographies of Stained Glass Windows* (Denton, Texas: Texas State College for Women Press), 1949.

Joyce Thompson, *Marking a Trail: A History of the Texas Woman's University* (Denton, Texas: The Texas Woman's University Press), 1982.

The Little Chapel in the Woods, Texas Woman's University, tri-fold brochure, no date

se window at the front of the Chapel reflects the colors of the surrounding countryside.

Eleven stained glass windows, each designed and executed by students in the late 1930s, adorn TWU's Little Chapel.

the subtly colored windows are beautiful and impressive—even to a two-year-old child who, 27 years ago, piped, "Look, Mommy, LADIES!" all over the Chapel in the midst of a wedding.

The rose window over the front door is an abstraction reflecting woman's joy in the physical world around her. The eleventh window, in the vestibule, is known as the signature window and shows the various builders, donors and decorators of the Chapel.

Architects of the Chapel were O'Neil Ford and A.B. Swank. Their associate was Preston Geren. The design of the Chapel was Ford's; his brother, the late Lynn Ford, crafted the altar, puplit and pews. Ford, Swank and Geren went on to architectural prominence in the world as well as in Texas.

When First Lady Eleanor Roosevelt came to dedicate the Chapel on November 1, 1939, most of the structure was completed, but the artwork was to come later. One stained glass window was set in place, with drawings of the others in position so that Mrs. Roosevelt could see what was to come. Work continued on the Chapel until 1941.
Continued on Page 14.

Clipping, Unknown newspaper, Winter 1979

The Chapel was built by the National Youth Administration.

NYA Officials .... Aubrey Williams, National Director, NYA; J. C. Kellam, State Director, NYA; Willard Deason, C. P. Little, Dan Dansby, Kay Alexander, C. R. Ledlow, Frank Hodges.

Architects .... Ford and Swank, Dallas.

Altar, pulpit and pews .... Lynn Ford.

Cost .... $28,500.00.

Funds for the Chapel .... $15,000.00 donation by Mr. and Mrs. W. R. Nicholson of Longview. Other contributions from students, ex-students, faculty members, and friends of the College.

Chapel Fund Committe of the Faculty .... Elida M. Pearson, Lura Mae Burton, Carlotta Corpron.

Student Chapel Fund Managers .... 1939-40 - Nelda Bell.
1938-39 - Catherine Pool, Molly Stinson.
1937-38 - Patsy Childers, Nita Hinds.

Chapel Committee .... Dr. L. H. Hubbard, J. Holford Russell, Jessie H. Humphries, W. E. Jones, Dorothy A. LaSelle, Constance Beach, W. M. Loveless.

Size of Chapel .... 90 feet long, 42 feet wide, 30 feet high.

Seating Capacity .... 170.

The Chapel is intended primarily as a haven for prayer and meditation but will afford small groups accommodations for religious services. It will be non-sectarian, but uniform in its religious appeal.

Dedication brochure, November 1, 1939

O'NFM_8

the National Youth Administration and unidentified photographers were displayed.

According to the George book "The task of translating ideas into something that could be built fell to Jerry Rogers, who did the working drawings for the chapel. The task was Rogers' because he knew the formula for the parabola so that drawing was viewed as a simple mathematical process (young builders of model airplanes at that time used the parabola as the shape of the standard wing tip)."[4] Jerry Rogers collaborated with Ford and Swank. Rogers later became partners with Ford from 1946 until 1953. George's archive at The University of Texas at San Antonio includes interview notes, interview tapes and transcripts with Jerry Rogers.

Construction

The "spreadsheets" were found in a project folder labeled National Youth Administration, voucher for expenses, 1940. The National Youth Administration photographs, construction drawings, and correspondence all provide documentation from the Ford collection which helped tell the story of the chapel's construction.

Research Evolution

Over the course of the six years that research has been conducted for *To Better Know A Building* exhibitions, archival practices have quickly evolved with greater emphasis on digital access through standardization, digitization, and acquisition of born digital content. This is a period in which innovations in the archival profession are working in closer synchrony with new research methodologies and user's need for data. Of late, fueled by urgency in part by the COVID-19 pandemic, archivists and librarians are responding to this information and cultural evolution with a surge in providing open access to digital content and ongoing development of international standards. Archival research is generally a slow process, but this is inevitably allowing researchers to quickly discover and synthesize the sum of the parts. Challenges in the democratization of information include building new data infrastructure, and focused efforts to balance intellectual property rights, privacy and confidentiality. As enablers of historical documentation, archives are also cognizant of practices in social equity around collection building and descriptive language. All require new monetary support and efficiencies through partnerships to widen global access. The future is ripe for new and exciting scholarly output using new digital platforms emphasizing data visualization and analysis. Digital scholarship also adds greater investment in the research continuum. Thus, the material selected for the exhibition was digitized for this article. With future classes making more frequent use of online teaching modes, the Alexander is partnering with the School of Architecture faculty to use its resources for graduate course content. In this, and endless new ways, The Little Chapel in the Woods and O'Neil Ford can serve as an influential model for global scholarship in the 21st century.

1 Mary Carolyn Hollers George, *O'Neil Ford, Architect* (College Station: Texas A&M University Press, 1992), 51.

2 Thomas D. Broad and O'Neil Ford, "Toward a New Architecture," *Southwest Review* 17 (1932): 226.

3 Thomas D. Broad and O'Neil Ford, "Toward a New Architecture," *Southwest Review* 17 (1932).

4 Mary Carolyn Hollers George, *O'Neil Ford, Architect* (College Station: Texas A&M University Press, 1992), 54-55.

The Subversive Modernism of O'Neil Ford

Brantley Hightower

Growing up in the North Texas suburb of Arlington, the landscape was flat and the architecture was uninspiring.

Yes, Louis Kahn's Kimbell Art Museum was a short drive to the west in Fort Worth and I.M. Pei had amassed a sizable collection of respectable buildings to the east in Dallas. But in between, there was little to tickle the imagination.

On special occasions my brother and I would pile into our mom's Buick and drive down Division Street past Six Flags Mall to Arlington's only Toys "R" Us store. As we drove in excited anticipation, we would pass a landmark that filled me with wonder. Just past the US 360 overpass sat three giant square toadstools. As near as I could tell, these umbrella-like concrete structures served no functional purpose. Like much of childhood, they were shrouded in mystery.

As with countless other suburban malls, Six Flags Mall fell into a period of decline and was demolished in 2016. By then, the neighboring Toys "R" Us store had been closed for years, and the mysterious concrete toadstools had been demolished. (fig. 1)

Some seventy years earlier and some forty miles to the north, O'Neil Ford was a promising young architect practicing in Denton, Texas. Along with his partner, Arch Swank, Ford had designed several residential projects before winning a competition in 1938 to design a small chapel on the campus of Texas State College for Women.[1] This project would mark a critical transition for the office as it proved that Ford and Swank could design more than just houses.

There is some irony, then, that The Little Chapel in the Woods was, in fact, so *little*. At less than 2,300 square feet, it was smaller than some of Ford and Swank's residential work.[2] Even so, their design imbued the chapel with a monumental quality that made it feel much larger than it was. (fig. 2)

The Chapel stands as a monument of the work of the hundreds of students who participated in its construction.[3] Because depression-era organizations such as the National Youth Administration (NYA) and the Works Progress Administration (WPA) provided the workers, the architects could call for labor-intensive techniques without adding to the overall construction cost. The resulting project represented a rare inversion where material–as opposed to labor–was the limiting budgeting factor.

Like the proverbial jewel box to which it is often compared, a disparity exists between the formal qualities of the exterior and the interior of The Little Chapel in the Woods. From the outside, the chapel feels familiar. Whether rooted in the simple Romanesque churches of France or the Mission Churches of New Mexico, the form and overall scale of the building place the chapel firmly within the historical continuum of small-scale religious architecture.[4] The chapel's exterior stone, quarried from the nearby town of Bridgeport, ties the building to its specific place as much as any other piece of local vernacular architecture.[5]

The interior, however, is something else altogether. (fig.3)

Subdividing the nave of a church into a series of repeating structural bays is certainly nothing new. This idea goes back to the earliest Christian basilicas of fourth-century Rome, but even if the primary organization of The Little Chapel is rooted in traditional church models, the formula is tweaked. Instead of the roof beams spanning between masonry arches supported on masonry pilasters, here the vertical and horizontal structural elements are subsumed into one continuous form: the parabola.

A parabola is the curve formed when a plane intersects a cone. The shape dates back to antiquity: ancient Greek mathematicians knew of it, while Archimedes, da Vinci, Newton, and Galileo all used parabolas in their work. Even as the parabola found many applications in physics and mathematics, it was not until the 20th century that architects and engineers fully embraced the structural potential of the form.

Superficially similar to a catenary, a parabola represents the most efficient shape for a uniformly distributed load.[6] It transfers forces to the ground in a single, continuous form. In 1932, six years before landing the commission for The Little Chapel in the Woods, Ford described the parabola as a "Line that ends in infinity, a static, moving, and beautiful curve."[7] He goes on to reference the parabolic vaults of the twin airship hangars of Orly, France.[8] Designed by Eugène Freyssinet and completed in 1923, the hangars received widespread coverage, including a mention in Le Corbusier's seminal book *Vers une architecture* of 1923 (the first English translation was retitled *Towards a New Architecture*, 1927).[9]

While the parabolic rib vaults of Freyssinet's hangars expressed their concrete structure, brick conceals the reinforced concrete core of The Little

Tri-Shell Sign, Arlington, c. 1957, fig. 1

Front facade, The Little Chapel in the Woods, Denton, ca.1939, fig. 2

Interior, The Little Chapel in the Woods, Denton, ca.1939, fig. 3

Chapel's parabolic arches. This updated version of ancient Roman *Opus testaceum* saved both time and expense: although centering was needed to form the brick arches, there was no need for formwork for the concrete as the brick served this purpose. In this way, Ford paired a modern structural form (the parabolic arch) with a traditional material (brick) to recreate an ancient system of construction (*Opus testaceum*) that used a modern material (reinforced concrete) to improve its performance.

This multi-level juxtaposition of traditional materials and craft with modern structural forms and techniques would become a reoccurring theme in Ford's career. The blending of vernacular materials and modern ideas would come to define Ford's work as he developed from an upstart young designer with little formal architectural training into the grandfather of Modern Texas Architecture.

As the construction of The Little Chapel in the Woods drew to a close, the promise of a new project brought Ford to San Antonio. Over the next decade, his office grew in size along with the scale and ambition of the projects it executed. When the opportunity came to design a new university campus, the office was ready.

Beginning in the late 1940s, Ford helped transform an abandoned limestone quarry into the compact academic village of Trinity University. The initial goal was to build a traditional campus organized around formal malls and quads, but the extreme topography of the site made this prohibitively expensive. As with The Little Chapel, Ford chose to combine modern and traditional elements to solve the problem at hand. Ford used Tuscan hill towns as a precedent, locating the

Front facade, Margarite B. Parker Chapel, San Antonio, 1966, fig. 4

more private residential dormitories at the lower elevations of the site while pushing the more public academic buildings to the higher elevations. Clusters of buildings were informally arranged to create a series of dynamic exterior spaces.

Many of Trinity's early academic buildings made use of the lift-slab construction technique. This method of construction allowed for the pouring of multiple floor slabs on the ground before lifting them into place with synchronized hydraulic jacks, eliminating the need for elevated formwork.[10] Although the university would eventually abandon this system of construction, the horizontal lines of the protruding flat slabs established the architectural vocabulary that defines the campus to this day.

As Trinity University grew, the campus reserved space on its western edge for a chapel for its students. Preliminary design work began in the 1950s, and after considering a variety of different approaches, Ford and his team ultimately used The Little Chapel in the Woods in Denton as a prototype for the much larger chapel in San Antonio. (fig. 4) With its minimal detailing, the brick exterior of the Parker Chapel (1966) is more streamlined than The Little Chapel (1939), but its overall gabled form certainly belongs to the same vernacular tradition. In San Antonio, visitors pass through a covered entry pergola that modulates the scale of the building to a more human proportion[11]. (fig. 5)

Inside, the brick masonry of the nine parabolic arches is painted white. Combined with the lightly stained fir wood of the altar screen and pews, the interior has a Scandinavian feel that recalls the work of Alvar Aalto. Just a few years older than Ford, Aalto sought to create a Finnish version of

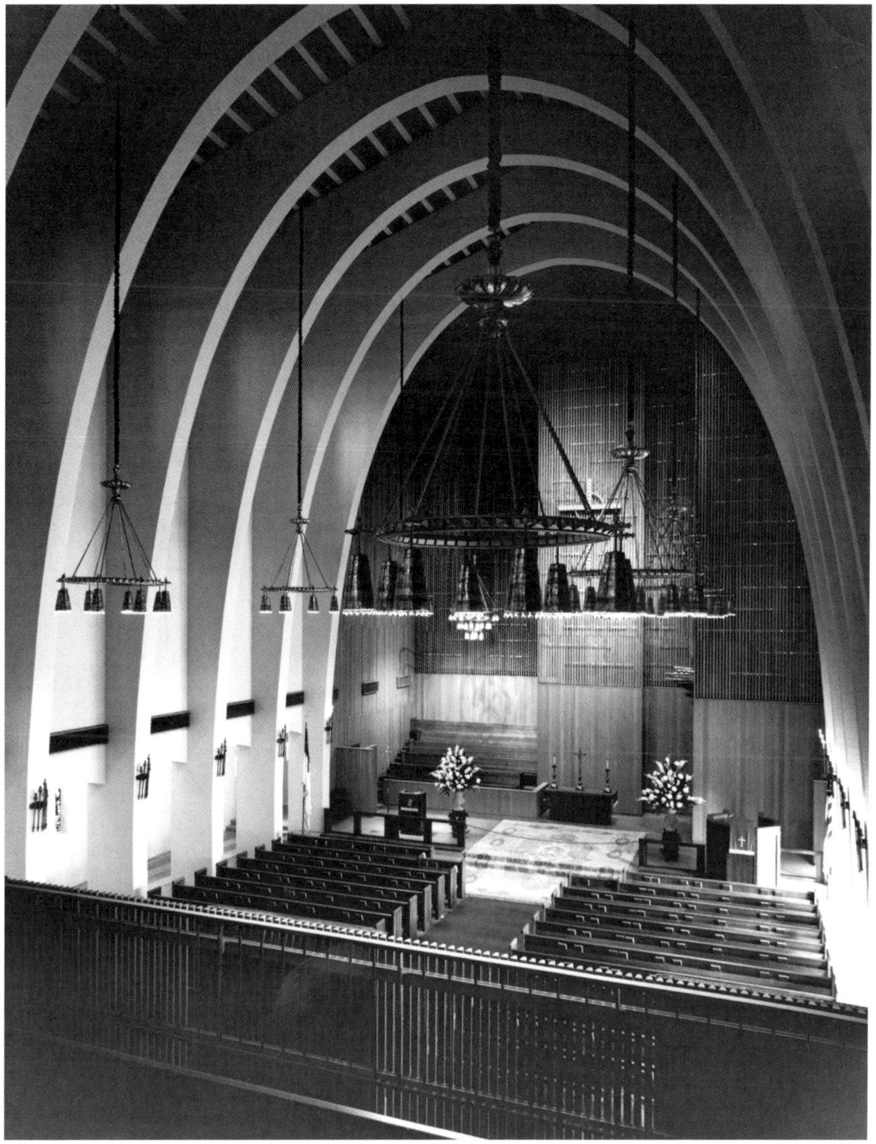

Interior, Margarite B. Parker Chapel, San Antonio, 1966, fig. 5

modernism just as Ford worked to develop an approach to modernism that was appropriately Texan.

Despite the larger scale of the Parker Chapel, hand-crafted details help humanize its interior.[12] From the elaborate hung light fixtures to the intricate chancel and rear screens, the chapel's *macro* modern structural forms find balance with touches of *micro* traditional detail.

To the north of the chapel sits an enclosed garden separated from the chapel by a series of art-glass windows.[13] These windows bathe the north side of the chapel in light, introducing an element of dynamic asymmetry lacking in the simpler layout of The Little Chapel in the Woods. Ford may have used his earlier chapel in Denton as a starting point, but he was more than willing to expand an idea when the opportunity presented itself.

Less than a mile to the east of The Little Chapel in the Woods sits the First Christian Church of Denton. The church opened in 1959 and so sat temporally midway between the Little Chapel and the Parker Chapel.[14] Like those other two projects, the gabled front elevation of the First Christian Church appears traditional. With its elemental form and subtle masonry detailing, the facade is straightforward and unadorned. (fig. 6)

However, as with Ford's other religious projects, the experience of passing through the facade is transformative. The conservative exterior gives way to an interior unexpectedly dominated by a series of thin-shell concrete forms. (fig. 7)

The unique structure that defines the interior of this church resulted from a collaboration between Ford and the famed structural engineer Félix Candela. Born in Madrid, Spain, Candela fought against Franco during the Spanish Civil War. After finding himself on the losing side of that conflict, he emigrated to Mexico in 1936. In the decades that followed, Candela became a pioneer in the development of thin-shell concrete structures. Using complex but structurally efficient geometric shapes, he minimized the amount of material required to enclose a given space. This modern approach to structural design attracted Ford to Candela, and the two would collaborate several times throughout their careers.

By the late 1950s, Candela had perfected a standard thin-shell structural unit, a "hypar umbrella" that could he could deploy in a variety of different architectural situations.[15] In Mexico, these umbrellas were often combined in multiple rows to create large warehouse spaces. In Denton, Ford and Candela arranged ten of these umbrellas in two parallel rows. They rotated the canopies of these umbrellas by forty-five degrees to create the church's gabled roof. They aligned the umbrella's supporting pillars to form an arcade that separated the taller central nave of the church from its two lower aisles.[16] Once again, Ford used a modern structural technique to recreate a traditional church form.

As singular of an architect as he was, O'Neil Ford was still an architect of his time. As with other designers of his generation, he was fascinated by the new, especially when it came to exotic structural systems that promised novel ways to solve age-old structural problems. This helps to explain why Ford was so attracted to the parabolic arch and the hypar umbrella.[17]

It is a curious footnote of history that Candela's first thin-shell project in the United States was located in Texas and was a collaborative effort with Ford. This pioneering project was not the First Christian Church in Denton, nor was it the more well-known Texas Instruments Semiconductor Building in Dallas. Instead, it was a restaurant in Arlington, Texas. (fig. 8)

With a suitably Texan name, the developer Angus Gilchrist Wynne, Jr. is perhaps best known as the primary force behind the creation of the Six Flags Over Texas theme park.[18] As part of his vision for developing the area between Dallas and Fort Worth, Wynne sought to create an "industrial park of the future" that linked road, rail, and air transportation.[19]

As with many developer projects, the stated ambitions of the Great Southwest Industrial Park were grand and, in retrospect, unrealistic. Ford was paired with a team of planners and engineers to propose a vision for the 5,000-acre development.[20] Ford reached out to Candela to design a standard thin shell concrete element–a hypar umbrella–that could be deployed individually as an entry canopy or arrayed in series to create large warehouse structures. As with the lift-slabs of Trinity, the intent was for these structures to define the architectural character of the entire Great Southwest Development.

After a temporary, full-scale mockup was built and load-tested in 1957, Ford added two of these hypar umbrellas to his design of the Crossroads Restaurant the following year.[21] These concrete toadstools found themselves incorporated into a handful of other structures, including a gas station, a hotel, and a sign for the Great Southwest Development that sat on the side of the road just past the US 360 overpass. As memorable as these structures were, the industrial park never

P.34 Front facade, First Christian Church of Denton, Denton, 1959, fig. 6
P.35 Interior, First Christian Church of Denton, Denton, 1959, fig. 7
P.37 Crossroads Restaurant, Arlington, 1958, fig. 8

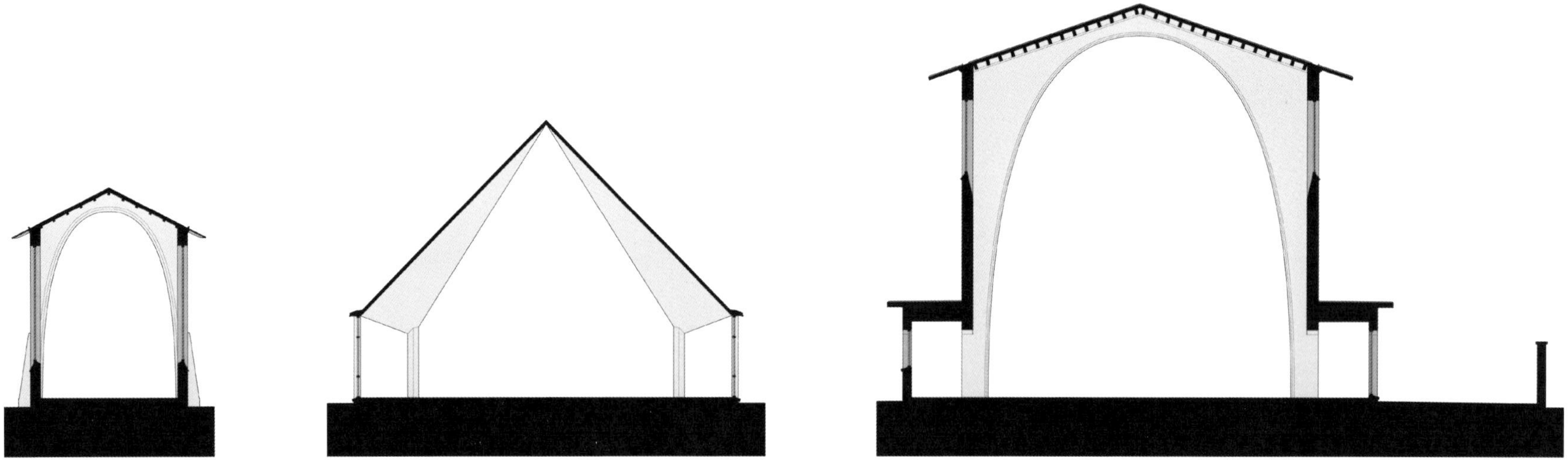

Sections, The Little Chapel in the Woods, Denton, 1939; First Christian Church of Denton, Denton, 1959; Margarite B. Parker Chapel, San Antonio, 1966, fig. 9

developed the singular architectural character of the Trinity campus. Standard steel-framed warehouses proved to be more economical to build, and in time all the grand architectural ambitions of the project were abandoned[22].

The complexities in the work of Ford's long and varied career can be difficult to recognize by outsiders. In the handful of projects discussed here, we see both the subtle reimagining of familiar historical precedents and more radical expressions of innovative structural technologies. For Ford, this was not an either/or proposition. Unconventional structural forms could be synthesized into otherwise traditional projects (i.e., The Little Chapel in the Woods and the Margarite B. Parker Chapel) just as historical building types could be recreated using radical structural elements (i.e., the First Christian Church of Denton). (fig. 9)

Ford's unique contribution to architecture in Texas was significant, but his ability to synthesize the new and the old is what gives many of his projects a surprising and often subversive quality. You do not expect parabolic arches inside a building that looks like The Little Chapel in the Woods, nor do you expect thin shell concrete hyper umbrellas inside a building that looks like the First Christian Church in Denton. By couching modernism in terms of structural efficiency, Ford was able to convince his clients to embrace more radically modern architectural propositions. In doing so, Ford pushed the envelope of modernism in Texas, allowing for the creation of an architecture that was just as modern as it was Texan.

1 Texas State College for Women renamed itself Texas Women's University in 1957.
2 Ford and Swank's 1938 Frank Murchison Residence in San Antonio was over twice as large.
3 Dillon, David. *The Architecture of O'Neil Ford: Celebrating Place*. Austin, University of Texas Press, 1999, p. 44.
4 Dillon, 42.
5 George, Mary Carolyn Hollers. *O'Neil Ford, Architect*. College Station, Texas A&M University Press, 1992, p. 53.
6 A catenary is the shape a hanging cable forms when supported at either end. When inverted, a catenary is the ideal curve for an arch supporting only its own weight. A parabola is the ideal curve for an arch supporting a uniformly distributed load.
7 Ford, O'Neil. "Organic Building." *Southwest Review*, vol. 17, no. 2, 1932, p. 226.
8 These hangars did not last much longer than the age of the dirigible itself: for as influential as they were, they did not survive the Second World War.
9 Le Corbusier. *Towards a New Architecture*. New York, Dover, 1986, p. 284-285.
10 The lift-slab construction technique was developed by the flamboyant businessman and adventurer Tom Slick, who also happened to be a member of Trinity's board.
11 A similar pergola was initially designed for The Little Chapel but it was altered to the simple vestibule that was ultimately built.
12 Many of these details were courtesy of Ford's younger brother, Lynn.
13 Unlike the multi-color stained glass found in most churches, the patterned art-glass windows found here is clear or translucent. The windows were designed by Lynn Ford in collaboration with Ruth Dunn.
14 St. Stephens Episcopal Church, located in southeast San Antonio, was Ford's only church project between The Little Chapel and First Christian Church. It was demolished in 2016 and replaced with a Mr. Bubble Car Wash.
15 Garlock, Maria E. Moreyra, and David P. Billington. *Félix Candela: Engineer, Builder, Structural Artist*. Princeton, Princeton University Press, 2008, p. 98.
16 These lower aisles are bathed in light by floor-to-ceiling glass inserted between the ground and the lower edge of the angled hypar umbrellas.
17 Dillon, 75.
18 Of the several theme parks built in the years immediately after Disneyland, Six Flags was the only park to achieve any level of success.
19 Dillon, 77.
20 George, 135.
21 Just as Arlington sat at the crossroads between Dallas and Fort Worth, the restaurant was intended to be a crossroads where the executives of the growing industrial park could meet to make deals.
22 Dillon, 77.

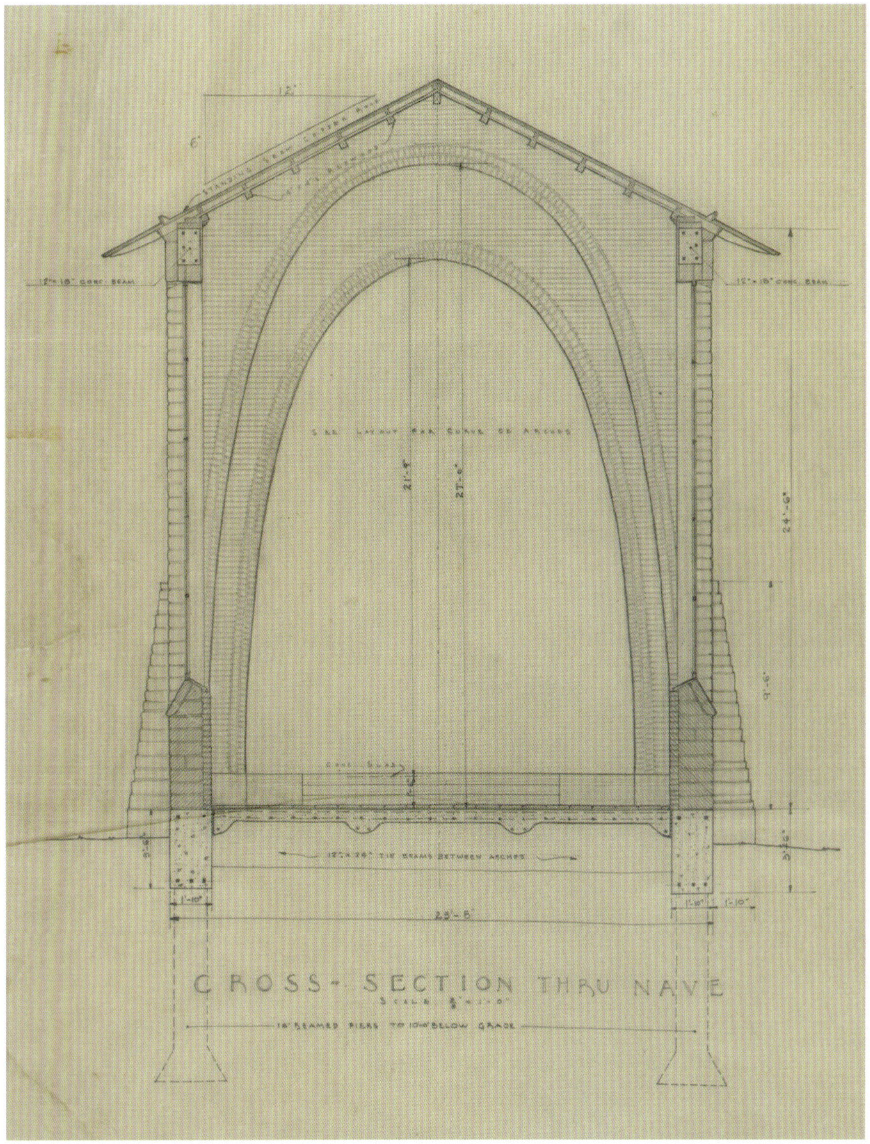

Cross-section through nave, from drawing no. 4, see full sheet on p. 99; O'Neil Ford, Arch Swank, Preston Geren (associate architect)

Making the Woods for The Little Chapel: The Native Landscape Movement and Modern Architecture in Texas

Kathryn Holliday

When The Little Chapel in the Woods opened on the campus of the Texas State College for Women in 1938, it was on a part of campus known as Lowry Woods and surrounded by the Texas Garden designed by faculty and nurtured by students. Native trees, shrubs, and perennials like cedar elms, red buds, oaks, thrift, asters, wood violets, and columbine combined with popular specimens like bachelor buttons and pinks to create a series of shade gardens, rock gardens, and flowering beds. A spring-fed fountain cascaded down a series of terraces formed by stone taken from the site, flowing toward a pond shaped in the form of Texas and filled with water grasses. Meandering pathways led from the campus to the chapel through the gardens and created what one student later called a "woody theater of stateliness."[1] The chapel was the final piece of a native landscape in development for a decade and should be understood as one piece of a larger effort to design an idealized, meditative landscape through artistic and scientific collaboration.

The specificity of landscape is essential to modern conceptions of regionalism, and it has shaped the way that O'Neil Ford's Texas modernism is interpreted. In his reading of Ford's work, architecture critic David Dillon celebrated his "passion for place" echoing the earlier polemics of Ford's mentor David Williams, who romanticized "the color of the land, the native flowers and trees, and the Southwestern sky."[2] Ford's collaboration with the landscape architects Arthur and Marie Berger to create the campus at Trinity University in San Antonio created one of the great works of modern regionalist architecture. At the urging of William Wurster to "let the hills design the buildings," the rugged walls of the old limestone rock quarry became the ground that rooted the terraced, modernist campus buildings in place.[3]

Beyond this regionalist discourse, historians have recently begun to revisit the role of landscape in modernist architectural practice.[4] Caroline Constant has emphasized "potential points of convergence" that deserve scrutiny as intersections of distinct ways of thinking about the meaning of landscape for architectural practice. In this context, the "woods" of The Little Chapel are essential to a deeper understanding of its significance as a modernist project meant to demonstrate Ford's approach to functionalism and organic building. As Kathryn O'Rourke has pointed out, Ford's understanding of nature derives in part from Frank Lloyd Wright, and his use of the term "organic" echoes Wright's emphasis on a harmony between architecture and site. Ford's landscapes are not the "architectonic garden" of Mies or the "genius loci" of Le Corbusier, and by looking more carefully at their context, we can enrich our understanding of American modernist practice as something more complex than a reductive regionalism.[5]

While Ford wrote about the Texas landscape as a valuable resource and inspiration, his attention was often focused on landscape as a pristine object of observation. His 1932 essay "Organic Building" profoundly reflects this dichotomous thinking, as he begins with a lamentation of "an unconsciously hostile attitude toward our environment, toward the land, which makes it difficult for us to build in harmony with the landscape," continuing that, "the obliteration of the land along with the frontier was a waste comparable to the casual and needless slaughter of the bison."[6] The essay though, veers to building technology and materials and focuses on the need for architects to use the materials of time and place, concrete, steel, and glass, quickly forgetting the centrality of the land to his own argument about the need for "organic building." Nature is something abstract rather than particular, a field upon which to build in harmony.

In Ford's best work, there is a resolution of this tension. The commission for The Little Chapel in the Woods, coming hard on the heels of Ford's "Organic Building," presented an opportunity to build with nature not as an untouched Eden, but as a carefully cultivated representation of an idealized native landscape. Denton in the 1930s was still a small town, but farms, highways, railroads, and university campuses had disrupted the native prairie of north Texas. The "woods" for The Little Chapel–the Texas Garden–were not the woods of the pre-modern landscape that Ford eulogized, but one intentionally created to idealize the connection between natural beauty and the appropriate setting for education, especially for young women.

The Texas Garden predates the chapel, and it was created beginning in the early 1930s, reflecting ideas from the burgeoning wilderness plant movement as well as more conventional progressive era beautification programs of ladies' garden clubs. These hybrid influences came from the collaborative educational environment

The Little Chapel in the Woods viewed through the gardens in 1940

of the university and its goals for its graduating students. The city of Denton and the campus of Texas Woman's University transformed under the leadership of university president L. H. Hubbard, who convened a campus beautification program led by three remarkable faculty members: Fred W. Westcourt, head of the rural arts program, Willie Birge, head of the department of biology, and Mary Marshall, head of the art department. Together they led the campus beautification committee to create multiple landscape projects, including a botanical garden and greenhouse and the "Redbud Trail" that connected the campus to Denton along a path of more than 2,000 trees. Inside the botanical garden, they also designed the Texas Gardens, supervised student workers who planted and maintained them and worked with the chapel committee to implement the chapel design.[7]

The educational environment at the college, which focused on training its graduates for employment in fields open to women, was the key link between these approaches. Under Fred Westcourt's leadership the Department of Rural Arts became central to training home demonstration agents in courses that included dairying, poultry management, floriculture, and landscaping.[8] The Cooperative Extension Service of the Department of Agriculture employed these agents to work with rural communities to improve land and home management practices during the Great Depression. Texas State Woman's College at one point graduated 40% of Texas's home demonstration agents, who had a multidisciplinary training in agriculture, homemaking, botany, and art that readied them for their mission to "prepare rural women and girls for modern farm life by clearly articulating a role for women as educated, productive, and forward-thinking."[9]

The program's emphasis on Texas native plants came from Fred Westcourt, who had graduated from the Agricultural Science program at Texas A&M in 1924, writing a master's thesis on "native trees and shrubs suitable for landscape purposes" in Erath County orchards southwest of Fort Worth. He wrote guides to native plants for Texas across his career, including his "Landscape Guide for Texas," (1948) and developed species of plants that could thrive in typical Texas landscapes, including strains of live oaks developed on the Denton campus.[10] His approach to landscape design is reflective of the approach taken at agricultural programs at land-grant universities as well as the native plant movements spearheaded by landscape architects like Jens Jensen and Frank Waugh. Jensen advocated for "native styles" that depended on native plants and informal design at the 1926 convention of the American Society of Landscape Architects and was at the center of debates about naturalism and conservation in Midwestern prairie landscapes.[11] Even closer was Frank Waugh, whose long affiliation with the National Park Service more closely paralleled Westcourt's lifelong dedication to shaping and maintaining the garden at the college. Waugh's development of design guidelines that shaped the landscapes of the national parks for decades called for the use of native plants and emphasized their ability to teach visitors about ecology and the natural beauty of the parks.[12]

Equally important was Willie Birge, chair of the biology department. Under Birge, the biology department developed a greenhouse, and students worked to classify and cultivate plants. Birge was also a leader in the Texas Garden Club, an organization formed in 1928 with its headquarters in Fort Worth. She was a charter member of the Highland Park Garden Club and later became a key member of the Violet Crown Garden Club when she moved to Austin in 1942 to care for her ailing mother.[13] She lectured to garden and women's club members across the state and emphasized the cultivation of flowers and gardens as progressive, productive work for women's advocacy in civic beautification. Birge's engagement with the Garden Club was also explicitly linked with the educational mission of the home demonstration agents.[14] Through Birge and Westcourt, the college became a frequent partner with the Garden Club in sponsoring public events on the campus that used the Texas Gardens and The Little Chapel as a demonstration of harmonious design. The 1942 state convention brought all the Texas Garden Clubs to Denton and *Southern Home and Garden* previewed the event, calling the campus "A Modern Tula!" somewhat remarkably comparing the deeply rooted sense of place and architecture created by the woods and chapel to the harmony of ancient Teotihuacan, with its blend of native plants, rich color palette, and beautiful temples.[15] Finally, Mary Marshall, chair of the art department, contributed an emphasis on modern art and an expansive view of collaboration in the arts. She, like Birge, was a graduate of Columbia University Teachers College, and brought a cosmopolitan and ambitious art program to the college. She actively participated in designing the rock garden, and it was Marshall who reportedly advocated for Ford

The path from campus to the chapel's front door was framed by a series of low terraces, limestone walls, redbud trees, and cedars. This photograph was taken November 13, 1949, well before the tower dormitories were built. Compared with the view on the next page, the formal beds are missing and the limestone path is now overgrown. From the Jean Hunger Traster Papers.

The Texas Pond, located in the gardens west of the chapel, 1954

By the 1960s, campus development encroached on the chapel's sylvan setting and jeopardized the gardens' future.

The Texas Pond, located in the gardens west of the chapel, 1954

Stone steps and terraces designed by TWU faculty and students defined the hillside connecting the chapel to the woods. Photograph taken 1959

to design the chapel, as she had known him while he was a student at North Texas State Teachers College. Ford would later design a house for her that still stands just a few blocks north of the chapel.[16]

When the chapel was added to the landscape in 1938, Dorothy LaSelle, professor of art and a member of the chapel committee, would later recall that, "the laymen and artisans who approved the idea of a building constructed in harmony with the site, and to fill the needs on this campus, seemed puzzled when neither Gothic nor Romanesque style were copied in the design for our Chapel." LaSelle continued to note that the architects' invitation to harmonize with the site provided the opportunity to "…[match] colors in glass with those in the sun-drenched countryside instead of imitating the hues of the Medieval glassmen."[17] In her interpretation of the rose window, LaSelle emphasized the links of the blues, greens, reds, and yellows to bluebonnets, Indian paintbrush, mesquite, and cactus as expressions of "woman's joy in the physical world about her."[18]

Beyond the site itself, the essential links between the Chapel and the garden lie in their emphasis on craft, scientific investigation, and practice. Just as the design of the chapel windows served as an opportunity for learning by doing, the Texas Garden served as an outdoor laboratory for design, teaching, and scientific research. While the stone borders for the pond, the rock benches, and cascades were set in place, the gardens themselves were never fixed or finished. Donations of exotic plants like cherry trees, donated by the family of a student from Japan, or bougainvillea, cultivated to amplify the southwestern feel of the garden, led to experiments in cultivating non-native species (neither thrived and only temporarily grew in the Texas garden). The garden also served as a source for cut flowers, both for students to use in floriculture studies and to ornament the women's dormitories. It was a space for progressive education and applied research that emphasized the same themes of women's ingenuity and accomplishment chronicled in the Chapel windows.

As Westcourt aged, Marshall retired from the art department chair position in 1948, and Birge left Denton for Austin in 1942, the gardens gradually fell into disrepair in the postwar decades. By the 1970s, the garden was so overgrown that even those who had walked its flagstone paths could not remember its form or boundaries. Alumnae wrote of their disappointment, including one who wrote to the student newspaper about the "desolate and sadly neglected stillness..."[19] Another writer "vowed not to return to campus" because her "beautiful memories" of the gardens and chapel had been "shattered" by the campus conditions.[20] The building of Stark Hall and Guinn Hall between 1965 and 1967, two dormitories of 21 and 24-stories respectively, radically changed the landscape experience and the relationship of the campus to Denton. They contributed to the neglect of the surrounding gardens and, ironically, embodied Ford's disdain for the "absurd skyscraper-building programs of cities."[21] But the towers also preserved the original footprint of the gardens until a restoration could begin.

In 1977, Texas Woman's University–as it became known in 1957–began a campaign to document and restore the gardens. J. Brough Miller, a professor in the art department managing the project, reported that he felt like an archeologist recovering a lost landscape. As bulldozers cleared away bamboo, the rock benches, retaining walls, ponds, and pathways were rediscovered and the full extent of the need to reconceive and restore the Texas Garden became clear.[22] Alumnae of the university donated generously to bring the landscape back to life, and with the leadership of university president and alumna Mary Evelyn Blagg Huey, the Texas Garden was rededicated in 1982 as a new generation became interested in the value of native landscapes as an expression of environmentalism and sustainability.

Today the landscape surrounding the chapel remains an essential part of its argument about modernist design despite the loss of its original design and extent. The restoration of the gardens in the late 1970s rediscovered its underlying structure but simplified its plant palette for maintenance, so it is no longer the laboratory it once was. A handful of Texas wildflowers, including winecups and columbines, are scattered in the shady rock gardens. As an experiment in the potential links between functionalist design, collaboration, and landscape, the chapel and gardens together fulfill Ford's vision of "…simple houses grown out of the soil" unbound by "rules of tradition" while also reminding us of the essential nature of landscape and native plants in the tradition of Texas modern architecture, transcending simple notions of regionalism.[23]

1 "Where are all the flowers?" *Daily Lass-o*, February 26, 1974; descriptions of the garden and its original plants can be found in Carolyn Ganner Burg to Mary Evelyn Blagg Huey, 25 April 1977. Fred Westcourt created guides to native Texas plants that provide clues as to the planting palette, including "Plant Material Native to Texas," an undated typescript booklet produced by the Texas State College for Women. All materials can be found at The Woman's Collection, Texas Woman's University.

2 David Dillon, *The Architecture of O'Neil Ford: Celebrating Place* (Austin: University of Texas Press, 1999), 2 and David R. Williams, "Toward a Southwestern Architecture," *Southwest Review* 16, n.3 (April 1931): 301. Though the essay was published under Williams' name alone, Kathryn O'Rourke has shown Ford's hand in writing the essay, see Kathryn E. O'Rourke, ed., *O'Neil Ford on Architecture* (University of Texas Press, 2019). Vincent Canizaro's collection provides an excellent overview of contested conceptions of regionalism in the twentieth century. Canizaro ed., *Architectural Regionalism: Collected Writings on Place, Identity, Modernity, and Tradition* (New York: Princeton Architectural Press, 2007).

3 Wurster, quoted in Mary Carolyn Hollers George, *O'Neil Ford, Architect* (College Station: Texas A&M University Press, 1992), 94

4 Caroline Constant, *The Modern Architectural Landscape* (Minneapolis: University of Minnesota Press, 2012), 20.

5 See Barry Bergdoll, "The Nature of Mies's Space," in *Mies in Berlin* (New York: Museum of Modern Art, 2001), 66-105 and see also, for example, Jean Louis-Cohen, *Le Corbusier: An Atlas of Modern Landscapes* (Museum of Modern Art, 2013): "If there is a blind spot in the astonishingly vast literature dedicated to Le Corbusier, it is certainly his relationship to landscape," 23. Other reevaluations include Jan Birksted, ed., *Relating Architecture to Landscape* (London: Taylor & Francis, 1999) and Thaisa Way, *Unbounded Practice: Women and Landscape Architecture in the Early Twentieth Century* (Charlottesville: University of Virginia Press, 2009).

6 O'Neil Ford, "Organic Building," *Southwest Review* 17, n2 (1932): 215 and 216. See Kathryn O'Rourke's excellent reading of the essay in *O'Neil Ford on Architecture*, 26-32.

7 The Woman's Collection at Texas Woman's University contains biographical information on the faculty members as well as several institutional histories that outline the role and purpose of the campus beautification committee. The narrative here is based on those sources, including a narrative by university president Mary Evelyn Blagg Huey, "The University Gardens," undated, but probably 1981. Histories of the university emphasize the importance of the Texas Garden and chapel for the university's identity: Joyce Thompson, *Marking a Trail: A History of Texas Woman's University* (Texas Woman's University Press, 1982) and Elizabeth A. Taylor, "A Summary History of Texas Woman's University, 1901-1971," Texas Woman's Collection, Texas Woman's University.

8 E. V. White, *Historical Sketch of the Texas State College for Women: The First Thirty-Three Years, 1903-1936*. Texas State Woman's College Bulletin No. 217, November 15, 1936.

9 Ann E. McCleary, "Rural Women and Girls in the Virginia Home Demonstration Program: Developing Leaders and Strengthening Communities," in Cynthia A. Kierner and Sandra Gioria Treadway, eds., *Virginia Women: Their Lives and Times* (Athens: University of Georgia Press, 2016), 184. See also *The Home Demonstration Agent*, Publication no. 602, U.S. Department of Agriculture, April 1946. The statistic for home demonstration agents graduated from Texas Woman's State College is published in White, *Historical Sketch of the Texas State College for Women.*

10 "Live Oaks to be Displayed at Convention," *Star-Telegram*, Feb.19, 1953.

11 Jensen quoted in Robert A. Grese, *Jens Jensen: Maker of natural Parks and Gardens.*

12 See Katherine Crewe, "The Rural Landscapes of Frank Waugh." *Landscape Journal* 22, n. 2 (2003): 126-39; Linda Flint McClelland, *Building the National Parks: Historic Landscape Design and Construction* (Baltimore: Johns Hopkins University Press, 1998), esp. 81-85; and Frederick R. Steiner, and Kenneth R. Brooks. "Agricultural Education and Landscape Architecture." *Landscape Journal* 5, n. 1 (1986): 19–32.

13 Little has been written about the Texas Garden Club and its influence on civic beautification. See Susan Allen Kline, "Texas Garden Clubs, Inc., Headquarters," National Register nomination form, listed 2011. The 1952-53 Handbook of the Texas Garden Clubs, Inc., lists Birge as a "Texas Life Member" of the National Council of State Garden Clubs and lists her as an authoritative speaker on gardens. Thank you to Susan Kline for this reference.

14 For examples of the wider efforts of women's clubs to beautify Texas, see brief mentions in Jean Andrews, *The Texas Bluebonnet* (Austin: University of Texas Press, 1986) and Gregory T. Cushman, "Environmental Therapy for Soil and Social Erosion: Landscape Architecture and Depression-Era Highway Construction in Texas," in Michael Conan, ed., *Environmentalism in Landscape Architecture* (Washington DC: Dumbarton Oaks Research Library, 2000).

15 "A Modern Tula! Definite Cultural Institution of the Southwest," *Southern Home and Garden* (January 1942): 5.

16 Dillon, *The Architecture of O'Neil Ford*, 27 and City of Denton Landmark Commission, "O'Neil Ford Architect, A Catalog of the Works of O'Neil Ford in Denton, Texas," 1992.

17 Dorothy LaSelle, "Director's Note: An Interpretation of Art Projects, 1938-41, Little Chapel in the Woods," undated typescript manuscript, probably 1982. The Woman's Collection, Texas Woman's University.

18 Dorothy LaSelle, "Iconographies of Stained Glass Windows," pamphlet produced by Texas Woman's University, 1949, 15.

19 "Where are all the flowers?" *Daily Lass-o*, February 26, 1974.

20 Marjorie Smith Moore to President Huey, 11 April 1977. Other letters with similar feelings came from Mrs. L. P. Chapman, librarian at Panola Junior College, 25 February 1977.

21 Ford, "Organic Building," 217.

22 Mary Evelyn Blagg Huey, "The University Gardens, Texas Woman's University," undated typescript manuscript. The Woman's Collection, Texas Woman's University.

23 O'Neil Ford, "Organic Building," 227, 228.

SPEECH IS A MIRROR OF THE SOUL AS A MAN SPEAKS SO IS HE

Women Who Work: The Radical Art of The Little Chapel in the Woods

Kathryn E. O'Rourke

The richness and power of The Little Chapel in the Woods, like that of many of O'Neil Ford's greatest buildings (most of them built at least twenty years later), lies not only in its architectural design, nor its embeddedness in its landscape, but in the interplay of architecture and the works of art within it. (fig. 1) The hand carved patterns on the pews, pulpit, bookstand, and altar; the narrow bands of mosaic in the vestibule and painted wooden beams; the globular metal chandeliers; and above all the eleven stained glass windows, together with the great brick-clad arches and brick floor, give the interior its singular luminosity. With their different materials, textures, and colors, the distinct works of art collectively make The Little Chapel one great work in the manner of the medieval cathedral, and place it in dialogue with the various strands of architectural modernism that aimed to integrate the arts–from the Arts and Crafts Movement to the Bauhaus–to the various international expressions of this ambition at mid-century.

It is nearly impossible to appreciate in photographs how small The Little Chapel is. As a consequence of the building's size and scale, the works of art within it are perceived with an intimacy and immediacy that is somewhat unusual in religious buildings. The catenary arches, sequence of chandeliers, and horizontally laid beams framing the altar lead the eye to the largest of the eleven windows, above the altar. In its harmonization of mass and lightness, and in balancing architectonic and painterly elements, the nave compels a special kind of quiet attentiveness, even before the viewer begins the process of "reading" the windows.

The story that these windows tell, and the story of their creation, is one of the most remarkable in 20th century architecture. The windows were first and foremost the fruit of a pedagogical endeavor, and the artistic program of The Little Chapel was deeply bound to the curriculum as well as to the broader education of the students. Led by artist and Texas State College for Women (now Texas Woman's University) faculty member, Dorothy Antoinette LaSelle, as many as 300 students, all of whom were women, participated in shaping and realizing the Chapel's artistic program between 1938 and 1941[1]. (fig. 2, fig. 3) They determined iconographies, set the style, designed the works, carved wood, researched glass making, and participated in the fabrication of the objects down to painting the windows and firing the glass in a kiln on the campus. Later in his career, Ford regularly worked with artists including Martha Mood, Beaumont Mood, Isaac Maxwell, Tom Stell, and, most importantly, his brother Lynn, to realize his distinctive interiors.[2] But in Denton, the artistic program went far further than those of later buildings. Informed by developments in modern muralism and Bauhaus glass art, it was ambitious by any standard. Beatrice Stebbing, one of the student artists, later recalled that her requests for guidance from stained glass artists were either unanswered or dismissed because the project was "beyond amateurs." The one encouraging reply came from Emil Frei, Jr., with whom the students met and who served as an informal advisor on window manufacture.[3]

The eleven windows may be read as one would a fresco cycle in which discrete panels with distinct subjects together comprise a unified work. While each window has its own title and subject, the theme for the work as a whole is *Woman Ministering to Human Needs*, which college president Louis H. Hubbard suggested. The eight narrow windows in the nave are each about 2' wide and 17' high, and are grouped in two sets of four: those on the left when facing the altar illustrate "Women Taking Care of the World" through the professions of nursing, teaching, social service, and science. Those on the right depict "Ministration to the Aesthetic Needs of the World" in allegories of speech, literature, dance, and music (fig. 4). The eight windows, along with the large chancel window on the theme of Motherhood and the signature window in the vestibule that tells the story of the building's creation, reinterpreted the traditions of ecclesiastical decoration and Works Progress Administration-era imagery to literally make visible the many kinds of work that women do, and have done historically, and drew attention to the challenges and experiences of exclusion that they have faced in the process.

Modern Glass and Modern Labor

In addition to their important place in the history of art in Texas, The Little Chapel windows belong to two developments in modern art in the U.S.: the renewed interest in stained glass that began in the 1870s and continued into the 1930s, and new artistic attention to the themes of labor and work, as they were carried in figural painting and

O'Neil Ford, Arch Swank, Preston Geren, LaSelle, and the student artists of Texas State College for Women, Little Chapel in the Woods, interior, 1939-42, fig. 1

Dorothy LaSelle supervising Billie Marie Culwell carving The Little Chapel pulpit, fig. 2

Beatrice Paschall making designs for stained glass windows, fig. 3

photography, such as in murals sponsored by the federal government, in canvases of the American Scene Painting and regionalist movements (including the Dallas Nine group), or in Depression-era photographs taken under the auspices of the Farm Security Administration.[4] In the late 19th and early 20th centuries–first in the context of the popularity of Gothic Revival style architecture and various iterations of eclecticism, and then with the emergence of the Collegiate Gothic style on many prominent U.S. campusesartists, architects, and patrons devoted more attention to stained glass than they had in perhaps 600 years.[5] Stained glass appeared in many types of buildings, and in 1903 the Stained Glass Association of America was founded; in 1906 it began publishing a journal, *The Stained Glass Quarterly*.[6] The vogue for stained glass continued for several decades, and also inspired books, such as the monumental text by master craftsman Charles J. Connick, *Adventures in Light and Color*, of 1937. Published by Random House with a foreword by a fellow of the A.I.A. and numerous color illustrations, this book, with more than 400 pages, catalogued the history, iconography, techniques, and practical modern concerns of stained glass. It was an important reference for The Little Chapel artists.[7]

Unsurprisingly, because most new stained glass was created for religious buildings, religious themes and figures were nearly always the subjects of 19th and 20th century windows. Works at colleges, universities, and research institutions provided a few notable exceptions. In Procter Hall at Princeton the Great West Window (1913) by William Willet and Annie Lee Willet is dedicated to The Seven Liberal Arts.[8] In the Gail Kern Paster Reading Room at the

LaSelle, and the student artists of Texas State College for Women, windows comprising "Ministration to the Aesthetic Needs of the World", fig. 4

Folger Shakespeare Library is the *Seven Ages of Man window* (1932) in which Nicola d'Ascenzo interpreted Jacques's famous speech from *As You Like It*. Perhaps the closest cousin to The Little Chapel cycle is the Great Window in the Thompson Memorial Library at Vassar College of 1906. It depicts Elena Lucrezia Cornaro-Piscopia of Venice, the first woman to receive a Ph.D. (in Theology, from the University of Padua in 1678; fig. 5). Below the central figure are allegories of Grammar, Dialectics, Music, Philosophy, Astronomy, Medicine, Geometry, and Theology.[9] Another extraordinary window dedicated to women was created for Bertram Grovesnor Goodhue's Christ Church Cranbrook in Bloomfield Hills, Michigan. This was the "Women's Window" of 1927, which depicted sixty biblical and historical women, including leaders in science, medicine, education, politics, and the arts as, well as "liberators" and "suffrage workers," including Lucretia Coffin Mott, and Elizabeth Cady Stanton.[10]

In some respects, The Little Chapel belongs to this group of important window designs, indeed in its arrangement of allegories of science, social science, and the arts, the eight nave windows broadly reflected the basic organization of the liberal arts and of intellectual inquiry in the West. And yet the windows of all of the other buildings were framed by tracery and their figures were rendered in a medievalizing style. The Denton windows departed markedly from both recent and long-standing traditions in stained glass with their resolute focus on secular, modern concerns (which was made more pointed by virtue of being set in a religious building), their explicit attention to work, and the artists' use of a figural style associated with social realist painting.

The windows' formal language not only differentiated them from other stained glass art but functioned as a vehicle for communicating ideas about labor because of the association of their modern, classicizing, figurative style with art that depicted workers. In part inspired by the Mexican muralist movement, and especially by the paintings of Diego Rivera, labor was one of the central themes of 1930s U.S. figurative art–whether in federally-funded murals, the prints of Ben Shahn, or the photographs of Dorothea Lange, for example.[11] The artists of The Little Chapel cleverly framed their depictions of labor in the familiar modern iconography of WPA-era figuration and within "safe" national themes of education, progress, modernity, science, nature, and public service. Like many other artists of the period, they did this even as they explored the interplay of representation, symbolism, and abstraction. With the Motherhood Window as its climax, at first glance the window cycle appeared to fit unthreateningly within a bourgeois patriarchal value system. The circumstances of the building's creation themselves seemed to reinforce traditionally gendered organizations of labor: outside young men employed through the National Youth Administration constructed the building, while women "decorated" the inside. This arrangement provided a certain cover to LaSelle and the students to not only focus on the politically-charged topic of labor, but to do so while repeatedly framing it in a feminist perspective. Indeed, it is only when one looks closely at the windows–their iconography and the text that is included in them–and understands them in relation to the interpretive notes that LaSelle published shortly after the building's completion, that the radicalism of the program is fully revealed.[12]

That text, *Iconographies of Stained Glass Windows*, appeared in 1941. It furthered the didactic program of the windows by explicating their imagery and reinforcing their feminist point of view. First and foremost, the pages identified by name the students who worked on each window and what their contributions were. The inclusion of this information implicitly acknowledged that women artists' names have often been left out of historical records and suggests that LaSelle attempted to forestall the possibility that that pattern would be repeated when historians came to write the story of The Little Chapel. Perhaps unwittingly, yet in the manner of modern feminism, in drawing attention to the multiplicity of artists involved, LaSelle, complicated conventional patriarchal (and capitalist) definitions of authorship that have tended to prize singularity over collaboration. Numerous photographs in the archives of Texas Woman's University showing the students working on the chapel confirm that the working process and the students' labor was highly important at the time the chapel was realized. (fig. 2, 3, 6, 7) In explicating the iconography, LaSelle often provided histories of the disciplines depicted that foregrounded the roles women played in shaping them. In some instances, she recounted the ways women were denied recognition for their accomplishments, or even punished for their work.

"Women Taking Care of the World"

Replacing saints with heroines of modern, secular culture, the artists organized the four windows that comprise "Women Taking Care

Studios of John Hardman & Company of Birmingham, England, and of the Church Glass and Decorating Company of New York Great Window (Cornaro Window), Thompson Memorial Library, Vassar College, 1906, fig. 5

of the World" around a single large figure that either represented a historical person or, in the manner of Rivera's depictions of peasants, workers, and revolutionaries, functioned as a typological representation of the profession or discipline–the "universal nurse," the "laboratory technician, chosen to represent Woman in the field of Science," and, in the window dedicated to teaching, the young Helen Keller and her teacher, Ann Sullivan. The artists gave voice to their subjects by including quotations associated with the subjects of the windows. Historically, quotations that appeared in stained glass were lines from religious texts. The presence of the quotations, along with documentary text, confirms that one of the artists' ambitions was to represent women's perspectives on work. Indeed, many of the quotations refer specifically to labor or to the dedication that it requires. Florence Nightingale appears in the Nursing window (Beatrice Paschall) alongside her words: "Nursing is an art; and if it is to be made an art (it) requires as exclusive devotion as any painter's or sculptor's work." (fig. 8) Other nurses pictured include Hildegard of Bingen[13] who, LaSelle's text recorded, "was one of the first to recognize the importance of scientific training, yet who was denied canonization by the Church because of her scientific learning."[14] Another represented the 17th century Dames des Charité who "were the first to give obedience in medical matters to physicians rather than priests."[15] Clara Barton[16] was also pictured and celebrated in the text for "having the plan for the International Red Cross Commission ratified by the United States Congress."[17] As a whole, the window celebrated progress in modern health care through the triumph of science and reason over religion.

Educator and founder of Mount Holyoke College Mary Lyon appears in the window dedicated to teaching (Ivy May Chollar). As if to emphasize the link between architecture and education that The Little Chapel embodied, she holds a model of Mount Holyoke's main building, although she is recorded as saying, "Never mind the brick and mortar; only let us have the living minds to work on upon." (fig. 9) Keller and Sullivan, and allegories of the senses that look very much like sleeping students, appear at the bottom of the composition. These figures allude to sensationalist theories of knowledge in which the senses deliver "the impressions that become our feeling and our understanding."[18] With the Nursing window and the Science window that follows, the Teaching window balanced empirical and humanistic forms of knowledge.

In the Science window (iconography by members of Advanced History of Art class, 1939; design and execution by Nora May Pierce, Mary Ann Chadick, Eloise Carriker, Beatrice Pascall, and Billie Marie Culwell; fig. 10), the technical labor of the laboratory and the theoretical work of science are both celebrated, as is the process of discovery. Chemistry, Physics, and Biology appear as allegorical figures. Flanked by two students performing experiments, Marie Curie's words contextualize the imagery, reinforce the idea of struggle in work, and, in the context of a women's college, read as a feminist exhortation against the barriers to achievement thrown up by patriarchy: "Life is not easy for any of us, but what of that? We must have perseverance, and above all confidence in ourselves. We must believe that we are gifted for something, and that this thing, at whatever cost, must be attained."[19]

The most politically charged and theoretically sophisticated window is the one dedicated to Social Service (Betty Winston; fig. 12). LaSelle's text introduced it with the claim that "one of the greatest contributions of woman to the betterment of humanity is her tireless effort to relieve distress and suffering wherever she has found it."[20] The window focused on two political activities–efforts by women to "improve living and working conditions through legislation to raise labor standards, promote safety measures, standardize wages, and limit child labor," and their work to "promote understanding among all peoples of the world."[21] This second endeavor was personified by the window's large, central figure who "appeals, by means of the radio, to all individuals segregated by race, creed, or nationality, to work toward a brotherhood of man."[22] Seen in light of the pronounced tensions between unions and employers in many parts of the country in the 1930s, the animosity that the creation of federal work programs inspired among some constituencies, the rise of radio-based propaganda, and the emergence of fascism, the window's de facto endorsement of a socialist agenda linked it strongly to the generally left-leaning, politically engaged art of the WPA, as well as to Rivera's major U.S. murals.[23] Its radicalism was heightened further by its setting, first and foremost in a chapel, and second in a small town in segregated North Texas. Near the top Winston depicted a "settlement worker as she leads two children, hand in hand, one a little negro child and the other a white child, symbolizing the abolishment of

Carmetta Drummond at work on one of the doors of the Little Chapel, fig. 6

Student cutting glass for a window, fig. 7

NEVER MIND THE
BRICK AND MORTAR
ONLY LET US HAVE
THE LIVING MINDS
TO WORK UPON
MARY LYON
HYGEIA

racial antipathies."[24] To appreciate the significance of this detail, one only has to recall the images of integrated labor forces and racial harmony that Rivera had painted in the fresco cycle in the Detroit Institute of Art and on the walls in the lobby of Rockefeller Center earlier in the decade. Although *Detroit Industry* (1932-33), with its depiction of a multi-racial group of assembly line workers in the Ford Plant at River Rouge, survived calls for its destruction, *Man at the Crossroads* (1933), in which a multi-racial group (including a nursing mother) piled its hands together in a show of solidarity as Vladimir Lenin looked on, did not.[25]

Elsewhere in her composition, Winston addressed labor and living conditions in gendered terms, using references to architecture. At the bottom of the window is a row of houses and two factory buildings meant to represent living and working conditions. Next to one factory "a woman and child, both laborers, are being lifted up by a woman social worker."[27] Adjacent to the social worker is a quotation by Jane Addams that linked human connection and work: "No two people or group of people can come into an affectionate relationship with one another unless they carry on a mutual task." (fig. 13) Winston interpreted Hull House near the top of the window. Between the quotation and the image were references to war abolition. The artist portrayed a "peace conference group" and "symbols of the settlement and the work it carries on to break down animosities between nations and individuals by wholesome community work."[28] Even as it was swaddled in the language of optimistic American grass-roots cooperation, coming at the beginning of the Second World War, and as the U.S. inched closer to joining the conflict, the window's pacifist message would have been as radical its pro-labor, anti-segregationist one.

The four windows that comprise "Women Taking of the Care of the World" entwined labor and feminism with modern science, medicine, and politics. On its own this was a provocative combination of ideas. As far-reaching in their socio-political argument as the individual windows were the arguments implicit in the title of this sequence–that care-taking is work, and that women do much of this work in the world. Economic theory has only recently begun to recognize how much labor, and especially care-taking, is uncounted and uncompensated, with the consequence that wealth is not only distributed extraordinarily unequally, but that it is dramatically underestimated.[29] The artists of The Little Chapel must have understood this intuitively, not only based on their knowledge of the world, but on their immediate experiences of working on the building's art in a process through which they undoubtedly gained much, but were paid nothing.

"Ministration to the Aesthetic Needs of the World"

While the practical, social, scientific, and political work necessary to sustain modern civilization was the subject of the windows on the left side of the chapel, aesthetic needs were the subjects of those on the right. In these, speech, literature, dance, and music were each represented by large allegorical figures that dominated the windows as their counterparts did opposite. Speech was dedicated to drama, oratory, and everyday language. Renaissance actress Isabella Andreini,[30] whom LaSelle identified as "the first great modern actress," was depicted.[31] Another reference to radio, "as a medium of expression, entertainment, and instruction," appeared as well.[32] (fig. 14)

The Literature window (Lucille Cudd; fig. 15) showed Emily Brontë [33] at work in a composition meant to acknowledge not only the writer, but in another allusion to the barriers women face, "any woman who writes in a secluded atmosphere, with many handicaps and usually without encouragement."[34] Near the bottom was a quotation by George Eliot,[35] whom the students selected to "represent all women poets," but also perhaps because her use of a pen name underscored the theme developed throughout the chapel of persisting in work in the face of social and structural impediments. (fig. 16) In another expression of the secular humanism established in the windows opposite, the Bible appears in this window, along with references to indigenous communication techniques carried in wampum beadwork and the machinery of modern writing–represented by a printing press and typewriter.

Religion enters the cycle in the Dance and Music windows. Isadora Duncan, Ruth St. Denis, Martha Graham, and Doris Humphrey are among the women honored in the Dance Window (Beatrice Paschall; fig. 17), which LaSelle's text described as showing women following their "desire to find an expression of beauty through movement."[36] She linked dance to religious experience: the inscription on this window is from a Psalm and reads "Praise ye the Lord–Let them praise His Name in the dance." The Music Window (members of Advanced History of Art, Spring 1939; and Mary Cook, Nora May Pierce, Betty Winston; fig. 18) also takes its inscription from

(L) Beatrice Paschall, Nursing Window, fig. 8
(M) Ivy May Chollar, Teaching Window, detail, fig. 9
(R) Members of Advanced History of Art 1939, Nora May Pierce, Mary Ann Chadick, Eloise Carriker, Beatrice Paschall, Billie Marie Culwell, Science Window, fig. 10

LIFE IS NOT
EASY FOR ANY
OF US BUT:
WHAT OF THAT?
WE MUST HAVE
PERSEVERANCE
AND ABOVE ALL:
CONFIDENCE
IN OURSELVES
WE MUST BE
LIEVE THAT WE
ARE GIFTED FOR
SOMETHING
AND THAT
THIS THING
AT WHATEVER
COST MUST
BE ATTAINED
NO TWO PEOPLE OR
GROUP OF PEOPLE
CAN COME INTO AN
AFFECTIONATE RELATION
SHIP WITH EACH OTHER
UNLESS THEY CARRY ON
A MUTUAL TASK
JANE · ADDAMS

"O MAY I JOIN THE
CHOIR INVISIBLE OF
THOSE IMMORTAL DEAD
WHO LIVE AGAIN IN
MINDS MADE BETTER BY
THEIR PRESENCE."
GEORGE ELIOT

religious language: "Gloria In Excelsis Deo," and depicts an organist, choir singers, a soloist, and a mother singing a lullaby to her child. Together the Dance and Music windows propose a profoundly humanistic, even sensual experience of religion, one far removed from the patriarchal structures of most organized western religion. With its references to motherhood, the Music window anticipates the subject of The Little Chapel's largest and most prominent window, set above the altar.

Motherhood, Landscape, and Authorship

At first glance, as the apogee of the cycle, the chancel window seems to undermine the feminist messages elsewhere in the chapel because it appears to reinforce the archetypical conflation of women and motherhood. And yet, seen with the windows that precede it, the tri-partite composition of the Motherhood Window (Billie Marie Culwell, Coreen M. Spellman, Beatrice Paschall, Helen Crain, Ivy May Chollar, Mary Ann Chadick, Dorothy A. LaSelle, Marilyn Yates, Lura Mae Kendricks; fig. 19) becomes legible as a radical reinterpretation of its theme. Where viewers might anticipate seeing a representation of the Virgin Mary (if they expect to see a woman at all in this position), they instead find a very ordinary mother and her baby and young child. The long inscription here is from the Book of Proverbs, and it emphasizes the domestic labor of motherhood, both in caring for people and tending to the work of a household. LaSelle drew attention to two sections–the ones whose texts were most visible from the pews–that explicitly refer to work: "She looketh well to the ways of her household and eateth not the bread of idleness. / She seeketh wool and flax and worketh willingly with her hands." In smaller panels are depictions of food preparation, sewing, gardening, and gathering flax. LaSelle repeatedly described the window as an illustration of different kinds of work: it referred to the "homely and unending tasks performed by mothers everywhere;" the "performance of prosaic daily" duties; time spent "working for the fulfillment" of the desire to have a pleasant home; the gathering of flax as symbolic of "any work, however menial, that the mother is willing to do for her husband and children" and referred to a "mother's leadership."[37]

To name motherhood as work, to place it alongside the professional and artistic work described in the nave windows, and at the same time to reinterpret Christian iconography in a chapel was to claim for women a place in the modern world of labor and to demystify femininity. While the chancel window did in some ways celebrate motherhood in socially conventional ways, as in the nave widows, it also reinforced the idea of persistence, which was often a sub-theme in WPA-era images of labor. This message was carried in the border of abstracted yucca plants that framed the central image. LaSelle herself determined this iconography (design by Marilyn Yates and Lura Mae Kendricks). She explained that yucca plants "symbolize vitality of heart and mind and resilience of spirit in women, qualities suggested by the plant. For, yuccas live where soil is dry, they grow and flourish in barren places. They find sustenance where none appears to exist, their roots go deep. Against the down-pull of gravity and the leveling forces of wind, in spite of withering heat, they grow up toward the light."[38] With this imagery and reference, LaSelle also evoked the challenging Texas landscape beyond the building, a landscape that the students, of course, knew well.

Together the windows were an exhortation to students past and future to carry on the work of those had come before them. LaSelle addressed them from the chancel and in the pages of her text, just as the student artists addressed them in the nave windows by intermingling history, biography, allegory, and very local, contemporary circumstances. The artists linked the theme of each window to campus life or learning in some way. For example, the campus health clinic appears in the Nursing window; in Science, students look into microscopes and study cell division and plant structure; the college's Administration Building is pictured in the Teaching window, while a reference to the campus publication, the *Daedalian Quarterly*, in Literature, was meant as a "stimulus to the writer on this campus."[39] Students appeared in Dance and Music, and in Speech they are shown working on set design.

LaSelle's yucca border anticipated the "Rose" window high above and opposite it. (fig. 20) Designed by Marilyn Yates, this window is an important early work of Texas abstraction. Fittingly, given that it is seen as the viewer prepares to leave the building, its allusions are to the Texas landscape, which the artist linked to emotional and psychological experience. The dominant color is blue, for the "rain-washed Texas sky or a field of bluebonnets,"[40] with hues of grey-green for mesquite and cactus, reds for Indian paint brush, and yellow for cactus blossoms. The interpretative text envisioned a parallel between Texas' unpredictable and often intense weather and a wide range of human experience: "colors

P.58 (L) Members of Advanced History of Art, Pierce, Chadick, Carriker, Psachall, and Culwell, Science Window, detail, fig. 11
(M) Betty Winston, Social Service Window, fig. 12
(R) Winston, Social Service Window, detail, fig. 13

P.59 (L) Members of Advance History of Art, Spring 1939 and Nora May Pierce, Speech Window, fig. 14
(M) Lucille Cudd, Literature Window, fig. 15
(R) Cudd, Literature Window, detail, fig.16

P.61 (L) Beatrice Paschall, Dance Window, fig. 17
(M) Members of Advanced History of Art, Spring 1939; and Mary Cook, Nora May Pierce, Betty Winston, Music Window, fig. 18
(R) Billie Marie Culwell, Coreen M. Spellman, Beatrice Paschall, Helen Crain, Ivy May Chollar, Mary Ann Chadick,Dorothy A. LaSelle, Marilyn Yates, Lura Mae Kendricks, Motherhood Window, fig. 19

PRAISE
LORD
GLORIA
IN EXCELSIS
DEO
TO THE WAYS
OF HER HOUSE
HOLD AND EATETH
NOT THE BREAD
WITH HER HANDS
SHE OPENETH
HER MOUTH WITH
WISDOM & IN HER
:: TONGUE IS THE
LAW OF KINDNESS
STRENGTH AND
HONOR ARE HER
IN TIME TO COME
HER CHILDREN
ARISE UP & CALL
HER BLESSED HER
HUSBAND ALSO &
HE PRAISETH HER
To Th GLORY of GOD and in Grateful Acknowledgment to Mr and Mrs W.R.Nichols

and forms are placed in the Rose Window which symbolize brightness and gladness, together with the brooding mystery of the Texas out-of-doors–qualities which ennoble and enrich the lives of Texas women."[41]

Although it is the first one she passes when entering the chapel, the final window the viewer is likely to examine is in the vestibule. It is the Signature Window, which depicts many of the people involved in the creation of the building. (fig. 21) Here Beatrice Pascall and Billie Marie Culwell inverted social and gendered hierarchies in the vertical organization of the composition. In the lowest register are the college president and donors. Above them, surrounding the chapel, is the Chapel Commission, with architects O'Neil Ford, Arch Swank, and Preston Geren at the top of the frame. In the next register, National Youth Administration workers lay stones and hammer while a foreman looks on. The largest single scene, comprising approximately one-third of the total composition, shows the student artists carving a chapel door, chiseling pattern into wooden surfaces, conducting the research that informed the windows' iconographies, drawing, and cutting glass. LaSelle, her back to the viewer, observes. (fig. 22) She is larger than the other figures and stands directly above the construction foreman. The window honors the many kinds of work required to create The Little Chapel, but, in keeping with the artistic program of the rest of the building, particularly celebrates the work done by women in the process. Like the interpretative text and the documentary photographs, the Signature Window was created to ensure that the story of the women who worked there could not be forgotten.

Marilyn Yates and Texas State College for Women staff, Rose Window, fig. 20

(L) Beatrice Paschall and Billie Marie Culwell, Signature Window, fig. 21
(R) Paschall and Culwell, Signature Window detail showing LaSelle, the students, and NYA workers, fig. 22

WORSHIP
THE LORD
NYA
WORSHIP
THE LORD
CHAPEL COMMITTEE
LOUIS · H · HUBBARD
JESSIE · H · HUMPHRIES
J · HOLFORD · RUSSELL
W · MARVIN · LOVELESS
WILLIAM · E · JONES
DOROTHY LASELLE
BEACH
ARCHITECTS
O'NEIL FORD & A.B. SWANK
ASSOCIATE, PRESTON
DREAMER
LOUIS HUBBARD
PHILANTHROPISTS
W.R. NICHOLSON
D · O · N · O · R · S
STUDENTS
FRIENDS

Diego Rivera, The Making of a Fresco Showing the Building of a City, San Francisco Art Institute, 1931, fig. 24

Glass, Labor, and Modern Art

While it is certain that the students were largely responsible for the designs and themes of the windows, it is also clear that the formal and ideological program of The Little Chapel owed much to LaSelle. Trained at Nebraska Wesleyan University and at the University of Chicago, and having traveled in Europe in the 1920s and 1930s, LaSelle was one of the first artists in Texas to embrace abstraction. In the decades after The Little Chapel was completed, she created a large and important body of abstract works. Particularly important to the development of the building in Denton, however, was the sabbatical she spent in San Francisco during the 1931-32 academic year. That year, LaSelle studied art with Ralph Stackpole and Maurice Sterne. Stackpole was one of the foremost artists in California and a national leader in the development of socially engaged figurative art. He was associated with the federal arts programs during the Great Depression and worked in many media, but was best known for *Industries of California*, the enormous fresco he painted at Coit Tower in San Francisco in 1934.[42] (fig. 23) His fresco was one of the largest among the twenty-seven on the theme of *Aspects of Life in California* that covered the walls of the tower's lobby, staircase, and second floor. With Bernard Zakheim, Stackpole had helped arrange the commission, which was the first mural funded through the Public Works of Art Project program. Twenty-six artists with nineteen assistants worked on the murals, and most of the people involved were current or former faculty or students at the California School of Fine Arts (which was later renamed San Francisco Art Institute), where Stackpole taught and LaSelle studied.

Although the Coit Tower murals were created after LaSelle's year in San Francisco, she surely would have known about them. The parallels to The Little Chapel project–multiple artists creating individual works linked by medium, mutually-agreed constraints and overarching themes, the implicit and explicit socio-political content, and the project's close connection to the pedagogical program of a college and to federally-sponsored arts projects–suggest that even if LaSelle did not model her work on the Coit Tower example, it likely served as a reference for how to integrate architecture, arts education, and experimental, socially-engaged modern art.

But even more significantly, LaSelle arrived at the California School of Fine Arts just after Diego Rivera completed one of his major U.S. murals, *The Making of a Fresco, showing the Building of a City* (1931; fig. 24), in the art gallery of the school. Stackpole had met Rivera in Europe in the late 1900s and visited him in Mexico City while he was at work on his major cycle in the Ministry of Education Building in the 1920s. Stackpole worked for several years to secure a commission for Rivera in San Francisco before he succeeded in arranging for him to paint *Allegory of California* in the stairwell of the San Francisco Stock Exchange, also in 1931, just before the California School of Fine Arts commission.[43] In *The Making of a Fresco, showing the Building of a City*, LaSelle would have seen a compositionally complex depiction of the many kinds of labor involved in architecture and construction, as well as a sophisticated interpretation of the labor of fresco painting. Like the interior of The Little Chapel, Rivera's fresco is concerned with the relationship

Ralph Stackpole, Industries of California, Coit Tower, San Francisco, 1934, fig. 23

Sommerfeld Residence, Berlin, 1920-1921: Stained glass windows designed by Josef Albers, fig. 25

Diego Rivera, Enrique Villaseñor, fabrication, Earth, Ministry of Health, Mexico City, 1929, fig. 26

Rivera and Villaseñor, Air, Ministry of Health, Mexico City, 1929, fig. 27

Fermín Revueltas, two windows showing workers building Mexico's national railroad from his series at the Hospital of the National Railroad Workers, Mexico City, 1934, fig. 28

between architecture and the non-architectural arts. At the center of the composition, on a *trompe l'oeil* scaffolding, Rivera created a self-portrait, but depicted himself seated and from behind. He is at work on the central and largest part of the tripartite painting, at the center of which is a giant, stoic worker, which, in the manner of the colossal mother in the Motherhood Window, dominates the painting and the room. Elsewhere on the scaffold, also with their backs to the viewer, are Rivera's assistants. The various people involved in the work of city building–engineers, constructions workers, patrons (who were in fact portraits of the muralist's San Francisco patrons), and, notably, a woman architect and her male assistants–appear in vignette-like scenes elsewhere in the painting.

Like The Little Chapel windows, Rivera's fresco melded typological depictions with evocations of specific people (portraits in the fresco; quotations and portrait-like renderings in the stained glass) to celebrate different kinds of a labor. In both instances, the artists enfolded a potentially controversial ideological program in an artistic one with a generally narrative character, and thereby forestalled the critiques that would undoubtedly have been directed at the works were they to have prominently depicted overtly political themes (somewhat like the political allusions tucked into in the Social Work Window, a small red star–a symbol widely associated with communism and socialism–appears on the pocket of Rivera's giant worker). Seen with The Little Chapel windows, *The Making of a Fresco* reads as a depiction of a decidedly male world of work. Notably, Rivera placed the single female figure in the fresco in a fully enclosed space. Her work takes place "inside," away from the "male" worlds of construction, engineering, and fresco-making, just as the artists in Denton worked "in" the building, while male laborers built it "outside." Creating art that generally conformed to gendered expectations of work (most industrial workers were men; most nurses and teachers were women) enabled Rivera, LaSelle, and their colleagues to depict politically-charged themes in ways that were palatable to fairly wide audiences.

It is possible that Coreen Mary Spellman, LaSelle's colleague on the faculty, also influenced the style of figuration at The Little Chapel. Spellman was particularly accomplished in printmaking, and designed the typography on the Motherhood window.[44] She taught art at the college from 1929 to 1974, and in 1932 studied with Carlos Mérida, a Guatemalan artist who lived and worked most of his life in Mexico. Like Rivera, in the 1920s and 1930s Mérida frequently depicted indigenous people as types, but to an even greater degree than the more famous artist, he used techniques of modernist abstraction, most notably pictorial flatness and color applied in large, clearly defined bands or sections–devices that translated easily to stained glass.

During the years that The Little Chapel was designed and built, LaSelle became interested in the work of László Moholy-Nagy after seeing Ford and Swank reading one of his books.[45] At LaSelle's invitation, the Hungarian artist came to Denton three times in the early 1940s, first in 1941.[46] The two surely talked about The Little Chapel project, and it seems likely that Moholy-Nagy would have mentioned his Bauhaus colleague Josef Albers' experimental work in stained glass. Albers had been a student in the glass workshop at the Bauhaus and was later its technical master while Paul Klee served as form master. There, in the early 1920s, Albers created a series of abstract works in glass, ranging from the small *Gitterbild* of 1921 to the stained glass window in the Sommerfeld House (1920-21) designed by Walter Gropius and Adolph Meyer. (fig. 25) His windows for the Ullstein Publishing Company building in Berlin and the staircase of the Grassi Museum of Decorative Arts in Leipzig followed in 1926-27. The most relevant possible precedent for The Little Chapel windows comes from the Sommerfeld House. Here, Albers filled tall, narrow frames with panes of abstract compositions of colored glass. In Denton, in the parts of the windows that did not include figures, text, or symbols, the artists similarly arranged geometric forms to create balanced, asymmetrical, non-uniform compositions. In both cases, rectilinear forms dominated, although they were not used exclusively. Peter Nisbet described the Sommerfeld stained glass as "a plausible intermediate stage between the sacred public environment of a Catholic church in 1917 [Albers' first glass project] and the lay public environments on which Albers worked in 1926-27."[47]

If LaSelle was aware of Albers' works, the Sommerfeld House project must have been particularly suggestive as an example of how to bridge the sacred and the secular in a modern idiom. Between 1936 and 1941 Albers exhibited his smaller 1920s works in glass in more than twenty single-artist exhibitions at galleries throughout the U.S., and it is possible that LaSelle learned of his techniques through one of these.[48] But whether or not Albers' work served as a direct inspiration, it is certain that the artists of The Little Chapel, like those at the Bauhaus were similarly motivated by an ambition to integrate the arts and to reframe the nature of labor. Beatrice Stebbing recalled that in the course of working on The Little Chapel, the students "had begun to feel as if we were medieval guild members working together, with a real sense of community."[49] Given the windows' theme, their setting, and LaSelle and the architects' interest in the Bauhaus, Stebbing's description calls to mind Lionel Feininger's famous woodcut depicting the Cathedral of Socialism, which appeared on the cover of Gropius' manifesto (1919) and captured the entwining of medievalizing and socialist impulses of the early Bauhaus.

Unsurprisingly, perhaps, the closest contemporaries of the Little Chapel Windows were not in Germany, California, nor even on another U.S. college campus, but in Mexico City, where artists had been depicting secular themes in stained glass since the turn of the 20th century. In the 1920s, in the context of the Mexican muralist movement, and as artists experimented with a wide variety of modern forms and techniques, stained glass artists in the capital began to treat a variety of social and cultural topics. Rivera himself designed four narrow stained glass windows installed in the new Ministry of Public Health Building (1929). Their theme was the four elements, earth, air, water, and fire, but Rivera allegorized each one using the imagery of modern work. (fig. 26 and 27) His compositions showed agricultural workers in fields hoeing and picking; sailors hoisting sails to catch the air; coal miners excavating the raw material for power plants; and a broad-shouldered shipman ready to crank the gear to pull a deep-sea diver back onto a ship. One of the largest and most vivid images of work in Mexican stained glass was the series of windows Fermín Revueltas designed in the Hospital of the National Railroad Workers in 1934. Here, he created modern, intensely colored depictions of multiple aspects of railroad construction and the people who undertook it.[50] (fig. 28)

Using techniques adapted from medieval traditions and modern muralism, through the windows of The Little Chapel, the women of the college spoke to one another, and to the students who would follow them, about women's lives. The cycle was one of the few, and perhaps the only significant work of art in the U.S. in the first half of the 20th century that insisted on the centrality of women in the world's major endeavors, and insisted that what women do when they are not at rest or leisure, wherever they do it, is work. The interweaving of past and present, of symbolism and representation, and the use of modern modes of figuration, conveyed both continuity across time, which was a source of strength, and asserted the modernity of the work and its message. That temporal interplay, the importance of hand-made works of art, and the centrality of education in the design and program of The Little Chapel in the Woods anticipate the ways these things also animated O'Neil Ford's architecture. In his early work in Denton, and thereafter, his buildings were shaped by his enduring engagement with the techniques and tools of modern industry, his devotion to craft and forthright expression of materiality, his life-long concern with education, and his persistent curiosity about architectural history, particularly of medieval Europe and Texas.[51]

The claims about gender and labor that The Little Chapel made were remarkable on their own, but they were all the more extraordinary when they are understood in light of developments in modern art. The windows are among the few, if not the only, examples in the U.S. of the use of modernist figural representational techniques in stained glass. That The Little Chapel artists created an interior that was thoroughly integrated according to a modernist ideal of unity across media further located the project in a critical current of art history; that they did so through a process of collective labor, with the Marxist undertone that it implied, made it even more radical.[52] Understood in relation to 1930s murals in San Francisco, Bauhaus explorations of the potential of modern stained glass, and significant works in glass in Mexico City, The Little Chapel in the Woods becomes legible not only as a major work of 20th century art in Texas, but as an important node in a dynamic, and perhaps unexpected, geography of modern art.

In Honor of Carolyn Peterson, FAIA

1 On LaSelle, see Katie Robinson Edwards, *Midcentury Modern Art in Texas* (Austin: University of Texas Press, 2014), 88-94; and Michael Ennis, "Thoroughly Modern," *Texas Monthly* (August 2001) https://www.texasmonthly.com/articles/thoroughly-modern/ (accessed 7 April 2020).

2 On Lynn Ford see Mary Lance, *Lynn Ford: Texas Artist and Craftsman* (San Antonio: Trinity University Press, 1978).

3 Beatrice Stebbing provides a detailed account of the artistic process: "Students Create Chapel Windows (With Just a Little Help from Emil Frei, Jr.)," *Stained Glass* (Summer 1996) 106-110.

4 On the stained glass in the U.S. see Albert M. Tannler, "'We only have one window:' stained glass and the Arts & Crafts Movement in the United States," *The Journal of Stained Glass* 28 (2004), 61-78. On WPA and WPA-era art see, for example, Richard D. McKinzie, *The New Deal for Artists* (Princeton: Princeton University Press, 1973); *Erika Doss, Benton, Pollock, and the Politics of Modernism: From Regionalism to Abstract Expressionism* (Chicago: University of Chicago Press, 1991); Carl Fleischhauer et al., *Documenting America*, 1935-1943 (Berkeley: University of California Press in association with the Library of Congress, 1988). On the relationship between Texas art and American Scene Painting see Francine Carraro, "The Texas Scene is the American Scene," in *The Art of Texas: 250 Years*, ed. by Ron Tyler (Fort Worth: TCU Press, 2019), 242-272; on Texas modernism, including the Dallas Nine, a group with whom LaSelle was friendly, but of which she was not a member, see Edwards, "Liberty and Lone Star Modernism," in *The Art of Texas: 250 Years*, 351-383.

5 On the history of stained glass in the U.S. and of women in it, see Betty Anne MacDowell, American Women Stained Glass Artists, 1870s to 1930s: their World and their Windows, diss. Michigan State University, 1986.

6 The Stained Glass Association of America was originally called the National Ornamental Glass Manufacturers Association.

7 Stebbing, 106-107. In 1939, as the design of The Little Chapel began, LaSelle traveled to France to study stained glass in Gothic cathedrals.

8 This window does include explicit religious text in the inscription at the bottom: "Nec vocemini magistri quia magister vester unus est christus" ("And be ye not called master, for one is your master, even Christ").

9 These closely resemble the seven liberal arts, which are grammar, dialectic, rhetoric, arithmetic, geometry, astronomy, and music. The window was created by the studios of John Hardman & Company in Birmingham England and Church Glass and Decorating Company of New York. See Charles Collens, "Vassar College," *The American Architect and Architectural Review* (Jan. 17, 1923), 53-54. On women depicted in stained glass see also Charlene G. Garfinkle, "Becoming Visible: The Coming Woman Stained Glass of the Woman's Building, 1893 World's Columbian Exposition," *Stained Glass* (Summer 1999), 108-11; 142; and Garfinkle, "'Becoming Visible' Revisited: The Coming Woman, Seal of Boston, and Women of Chelsea Stained Glass Windows from the 1893 Woman's Building," *Stained Glass* (Winter 2017), 54-59.

10 On the window, see Linda M. Johnson, "The Divine Sarah and the Women's Window at Christ Church Cranbrook," *The Stained Glass Quarterly*, vol. 106, no. 4 (Winter 2011): 294-298; 306; and "Women's Window, Christ Church Cranbrook," Michigan Stained Glass Census; accessed online: http://www.michiganstainedglass.org/collections/window.php?id=17-81-33 (11 Feb., 2020).

11 See Anthony W. Lee, *Painting on the Left: Diego Rivera, Radical Politics, and San Francisco's Public Murals* (Berkeley: University of California Press, 1999).

12 *Iconographies of Stained Glass Windows, Little Chapel-In-The-Woods, Texas State College for Women, Denton, Texas*, ed. by Dorothy A. LaSelle (Denton, Texas: Texas State College for Women), 1941.

13 1098-1179.

14 Ibid., 1.

15 Ibid., 1-2.

16 1821-1912.

17 Ibid., 2.

18 Ibid., 3.

19 Ibid., 4.

20 Ibid., 5.

21 Ibid., 5.

22 Ibid., 5.

23 For accounts of WPA artists' activities see *WPA: Art for the Millions*, ed. by Francis V. O'Connor (Boston: New York Graphic Society, Ltd., 1975); on Rivera's work at Rockefeller Center, Catha Paquette, *At the Crossroads: Diego Rivera and his Patron at MoMA, Rockefeller Center, and the Palace of Fine Arts* (Austin: University of Texas Press, 2017), 93-216; and on his murals in Detroit: Max Kozloff, "The Rivera Frescoes of Modern Industry at the Detroit Institute of Arts: Proletarian Art under Capitalist Patronage, "*Artforum*, vol. 12, no. 3 (Nov. 1973) 58-63; on labor imagery and, particularly gender, see Laura Hapke, *Labor's Canvas: American Working-Class History and the WPA Art of the 1930s* (Newcastle, UK: Cambridge Scholars Publishing, 2008).

24 *Iconographies of Stained Glass Windows*, 5. Later in his career Ford spoke forcefully in favor of integration. See, for example, Ford, "The Condition of Architecture," (1964), reprinted in O'Neil Ford on Architecture, ed. by Kathryn E. O'Rourke (Austin: University of Texas Press, 2019) 125-126.

25 On the controversies these and other murals generated see Ana Indych-López, "Mexican Muralism in the United States: Controversies, Paradoxes, and Publics," in *Mexican Muralism: a Critical History*, ed. by Alejandro Anreus, Robin Adèle Greely, and Leonard Folgarait (Berkeley: University of California Press, 2012): 208-226.

27 *Iconographies of Stained Glass Windows*, 5

28 Ibid., 5.

29 See, for example, Lourdes Beneria, Günseli Berik, and Maria S. Floro, Gender, *Development and Globalization: Economics as if All People Mattered*, second ed. (London: Routledge, 2015), and Nancy Folbre, "Measuring Care: Gender, Empowerment, and the Care Economy," *Journal of Human Development*, vol. 6, no. 2 (2006), 183-199.

30 1562-1604.

31 *Iconographies of Stained Glass Windows*, 6.

32 Ibid., 6.

33 1818-1848.

34 Ibid., 7.

35 actually Mary Anne Evans, 1819-1880.

36 Ibid., 8.

37 Ibid., 10-11.

38 bid., 12

39 Ibid., 7.

40 Ibid., 13.

41 Ibid., 15.

42 On *Industries of California* see Lee, 149-151; on the Coit Tower mural projects see Lee, 138-159.

43 *Allegory of California* was Rivera's first U.S. mural. On Rivera, Stackpole, and Rivera's work in San Francisco, see Desmond Rochfort, *Mexican Muralists: Orozco, Rivera, Siqueiros* (San Francisco: Chronicle Books, 1993): 123-126, and Lee, 88-105.

44 On Spellman see Edwards, *Midcentury Modern Art in Texas*, 39, 54, 89.

45 Michael Ennis, "Thoroughly Modern," *Texas Monthly* (August 2001) https://www.texasmonthly.com/articles/thoroughly-modern/ (accessed 7 April 2020).

46 He taught at the college in 1942 and 1944.

47 Peter Nisbet, "Josef Albers Lattice Picture. 1921," in *Bauhaus 1919-1933: Workshops for Modernity*, ed. by Barry Bergdoll and Leah Dickerman (New York: Museum of Modern Art, New York, 2009): 94.

48 On Albers' smaller glass works see *Josef Albers: Glass, Color, and Light* (New York: Guggenheim Museum Publications, 1994).

49 Stebbing, 108.

50 On 20th century stained glass in Mexico see Carla Zurián de la Fuente, "Liquid Walls: Stained Glass in Mexican Art, 1900-1935," trans. David A. Auerbach, *Journal of Decorative and Propaganda Arts* 26, (2010): 12-43; *Vitrales de México* (Mexico City: Secretaría de Educación Pública; Comisión Nacional de Libros Texto Gratuitos, 2004).

51 On these themes in Ford's work see O'Rourke "The Language of O'Neil Ford," in *O'Neil Ford on Architecture*, 3-46.

52 Jennifer Jolly has documented the way Marxist ideology informed David Alfaro Siqueiros's collective practices of art making, for example: "Art of the Collective: David Alfaro Siqueiros, Josep Renau and Their Collaboration at the Mexican Electricians' Syndicate," *Oxford Art Journal*, vol. 31, no. 1 (2008): 131-151.

Etchings, Sketches & Doodles

Etching, O'Neil Ford, location unknown, undated

Etching, O'Neil Ford, location unknown, undated

Etching, O'Neil Ford, location unknown, undated

Etching, O'Neil Ford, location unknown, undated

Etching, O'Neil Ford, "Backyard" San Antonio

Sketch, O'Neil Ford, San Antonio, 1926

Sketch, O'Neil Ford, Fredericksburg, 1928

Sketch, O'Neil Ford, Austin, 1926

Sketch, O'Neil Ford, San Antonio, undated

O'NFM_8

Sketch, O'Neil Ford, location unknown, undated

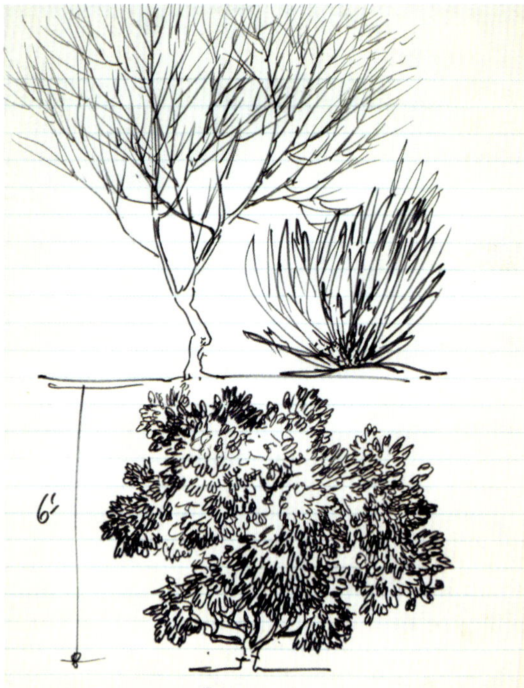

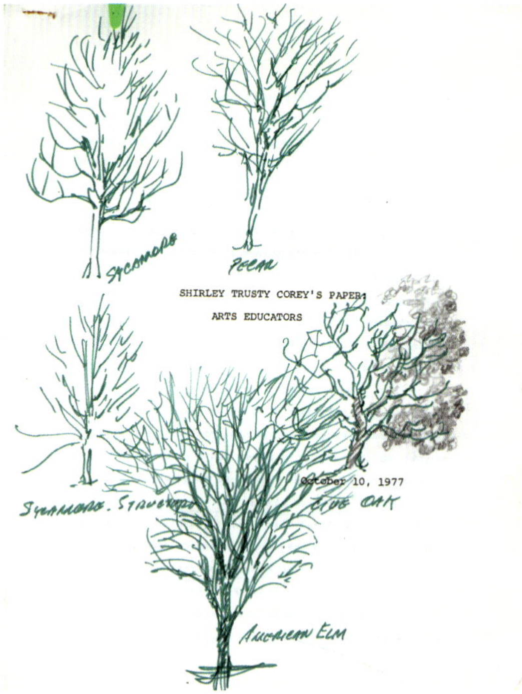

Doodles, O'Neil Ford, undated

Doodles, O'Neil Ford, undated

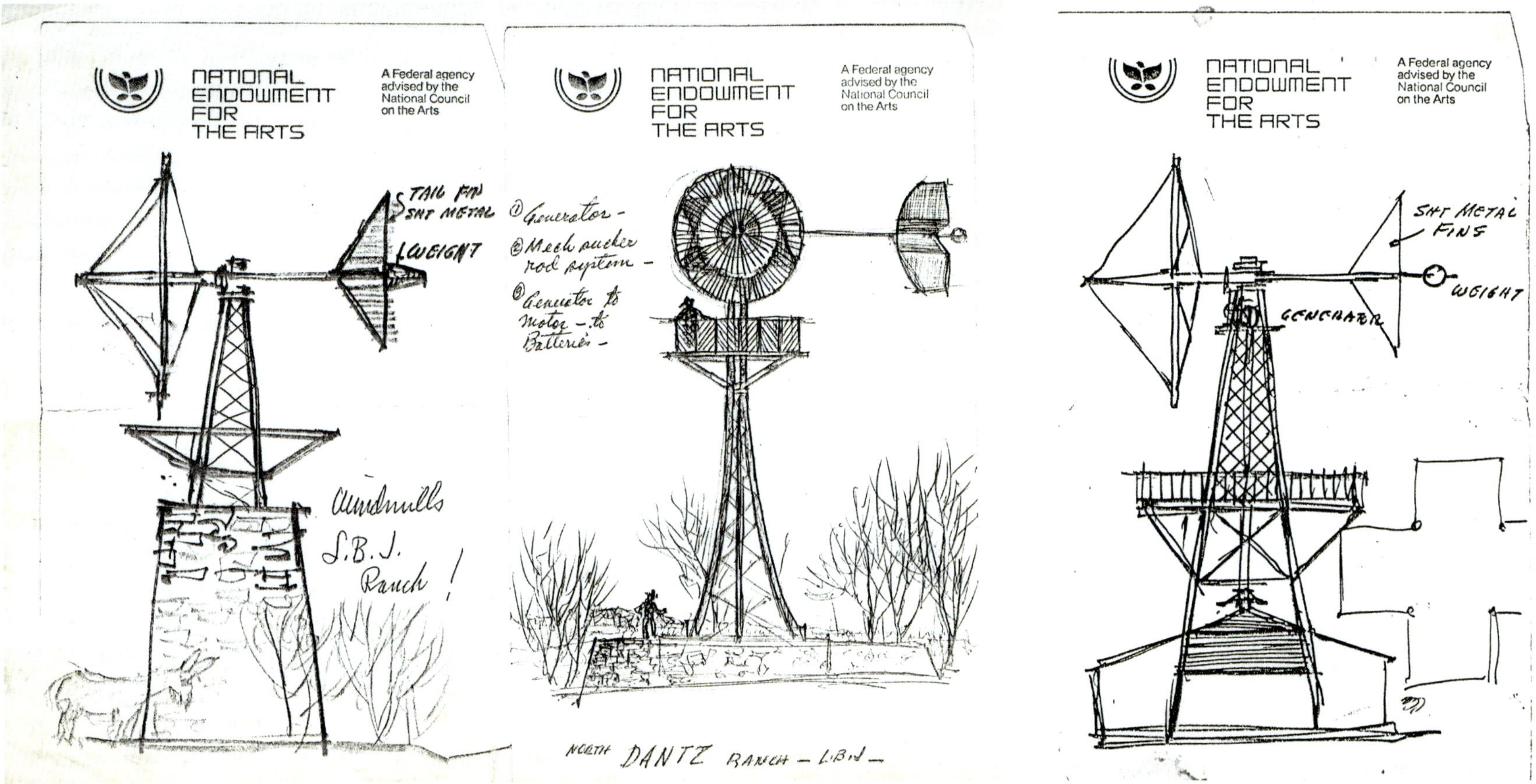

Doodles, O'Neil Ford, undated

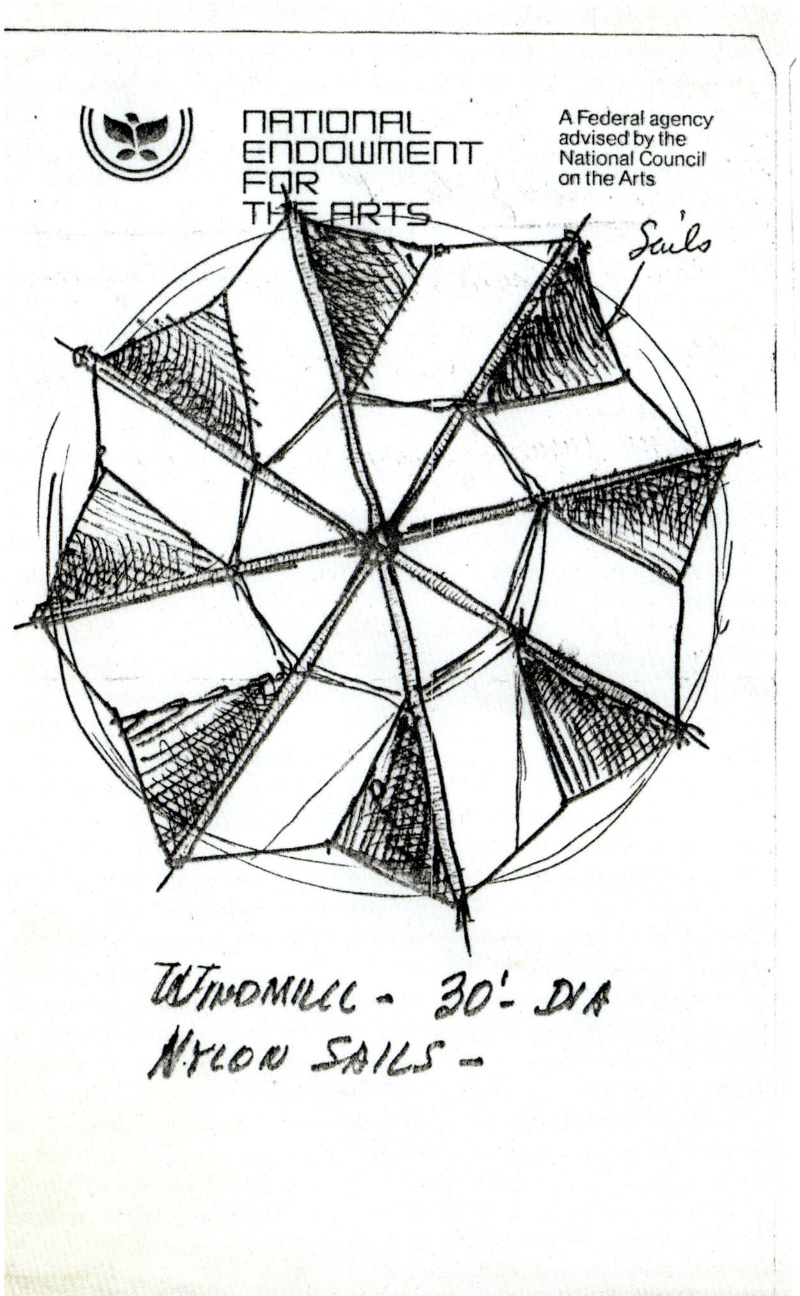

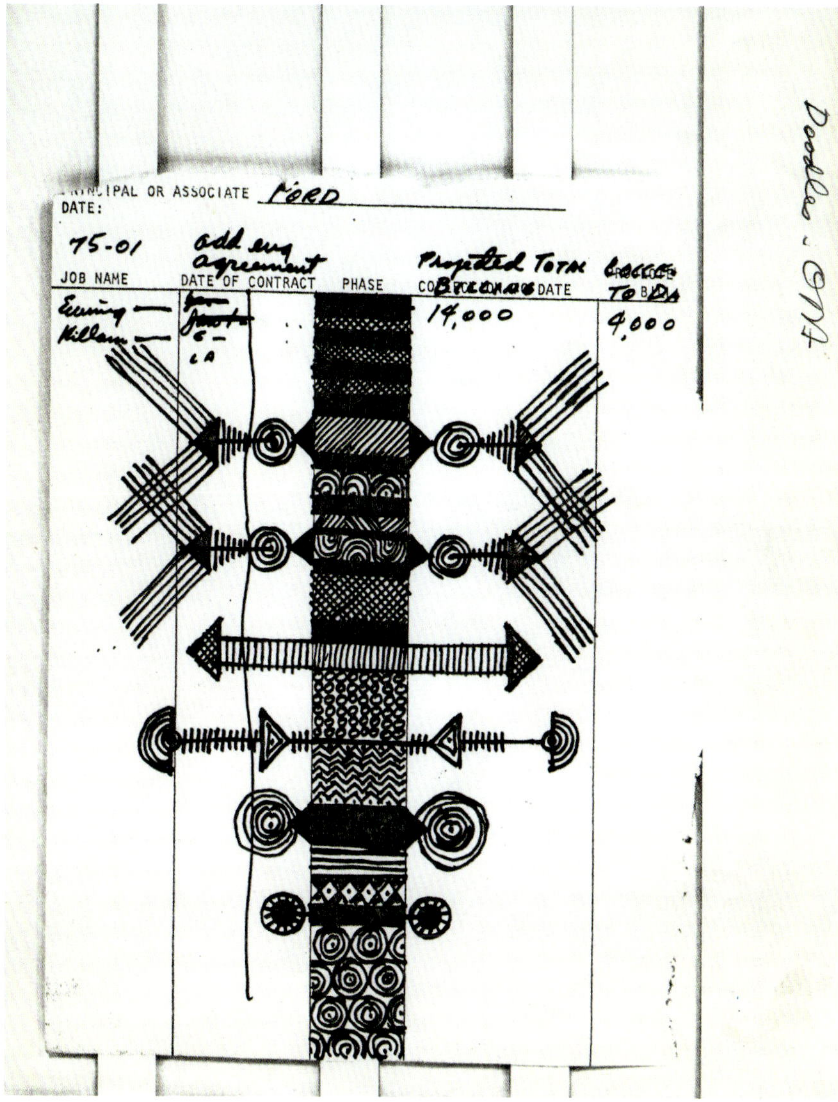

Doodles, O'Neil Ford, undated

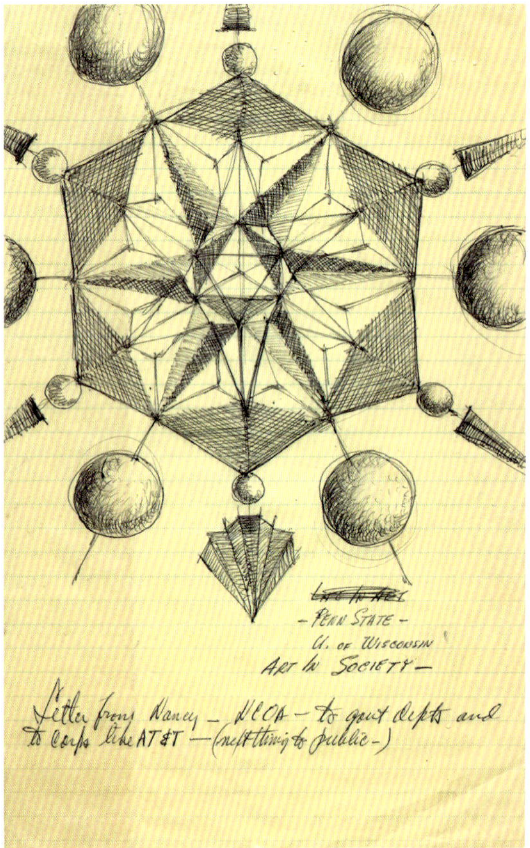

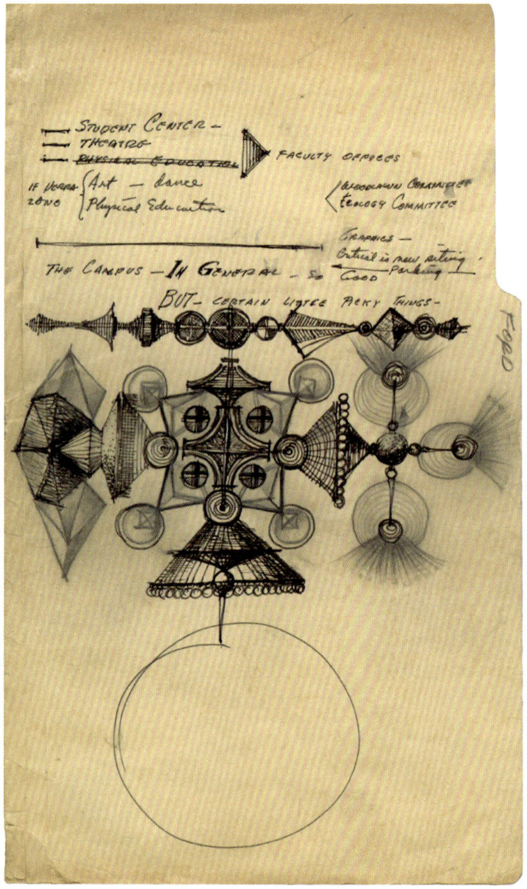

Doodles, O'Neil Ford, undated

 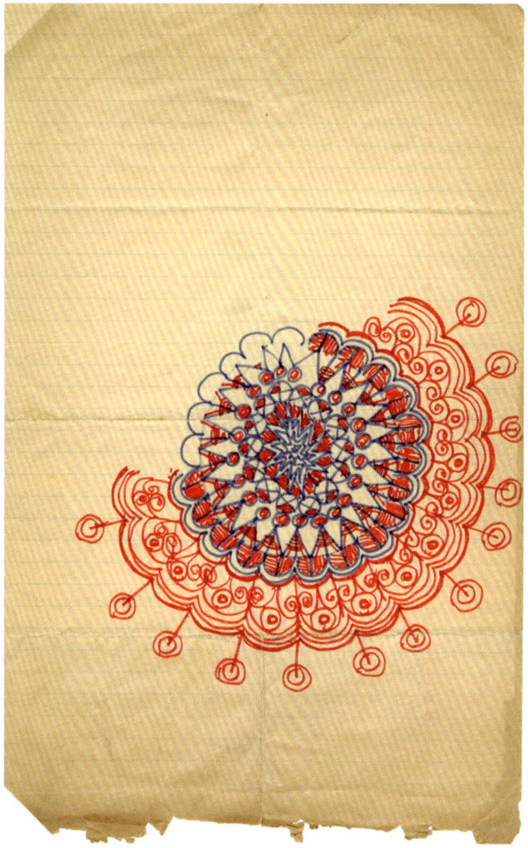 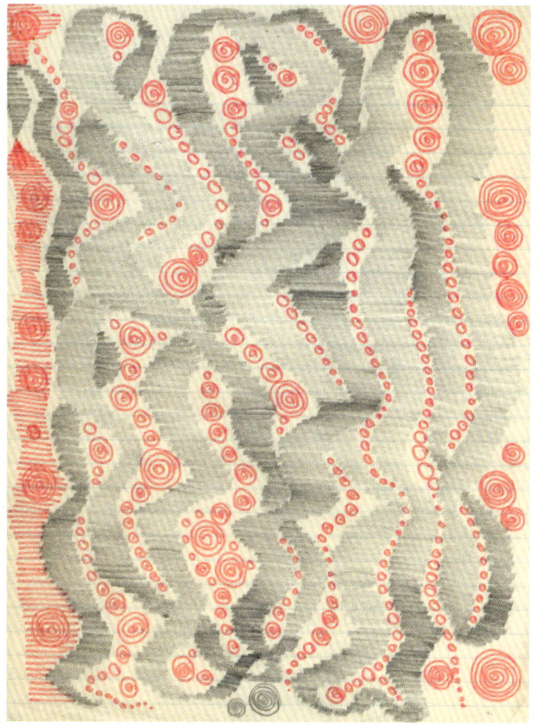

Doodles, O'Neil Ford, undated

Doodles, O'Neil Ford, undated

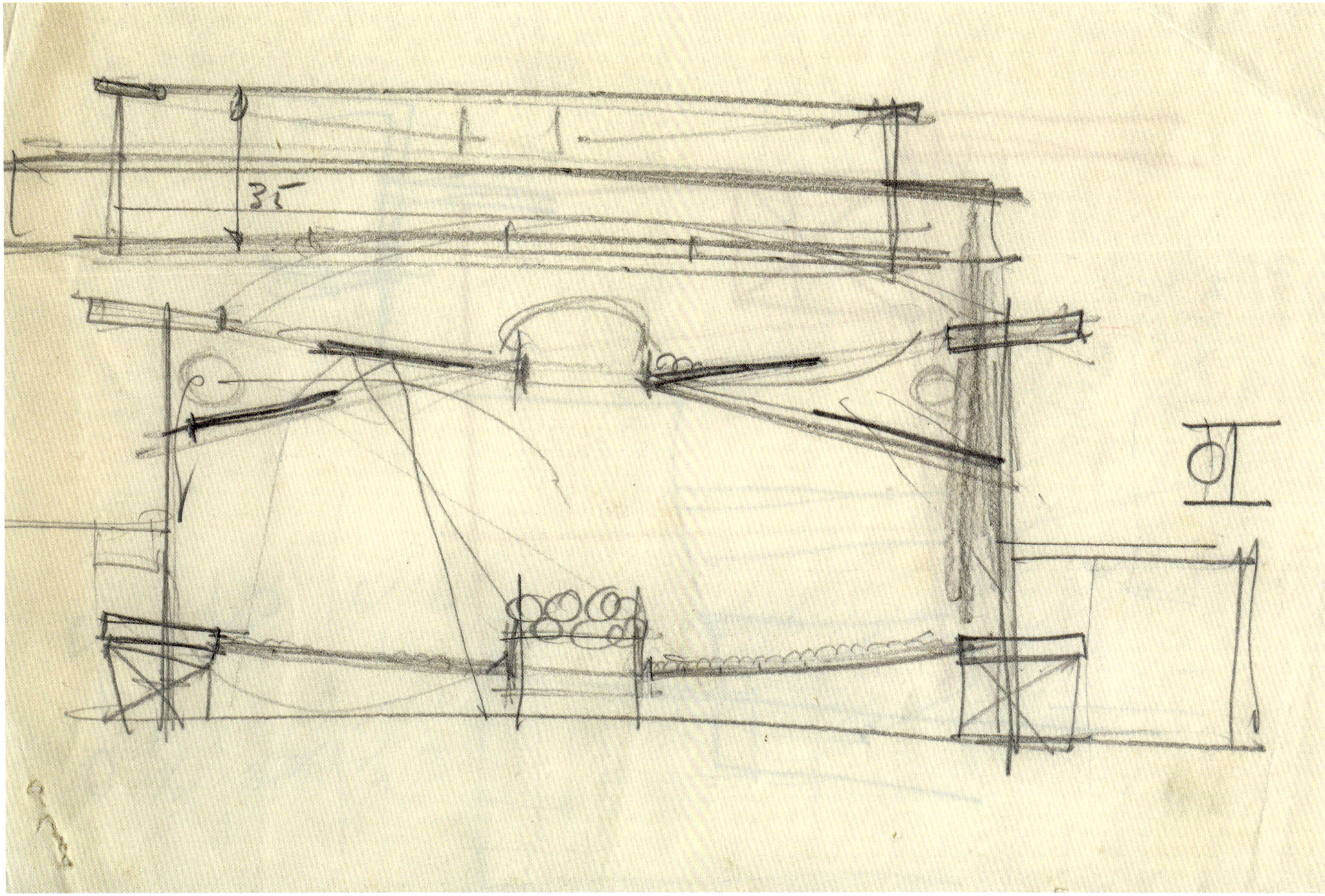

Sketch of the bicycle wheel structural system for the Villita Assembly Hall, O'Neil Ford, San Antonio, ca. 1960

Drawings, O'Neil Ford, undated

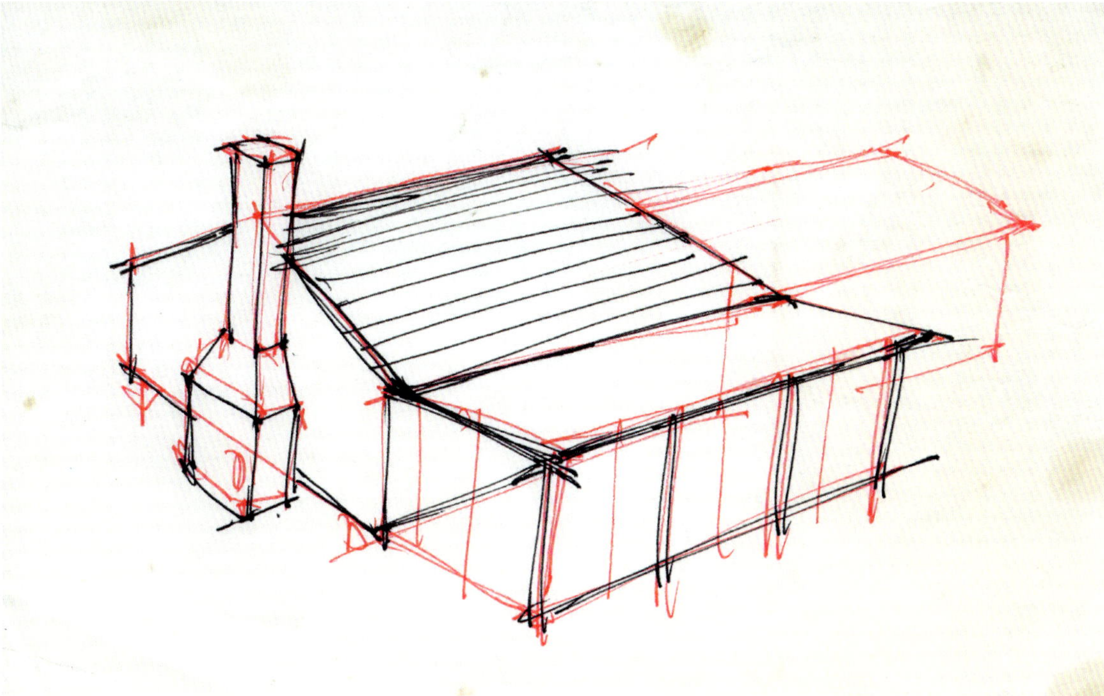

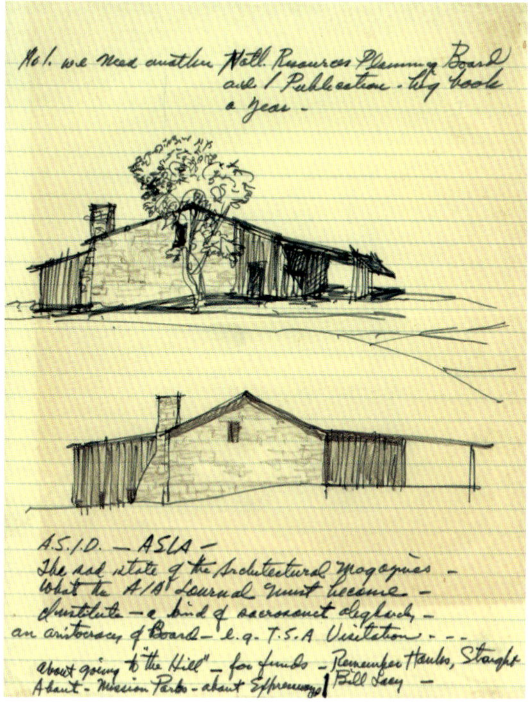

Sketches, O'Neil Ford, undated

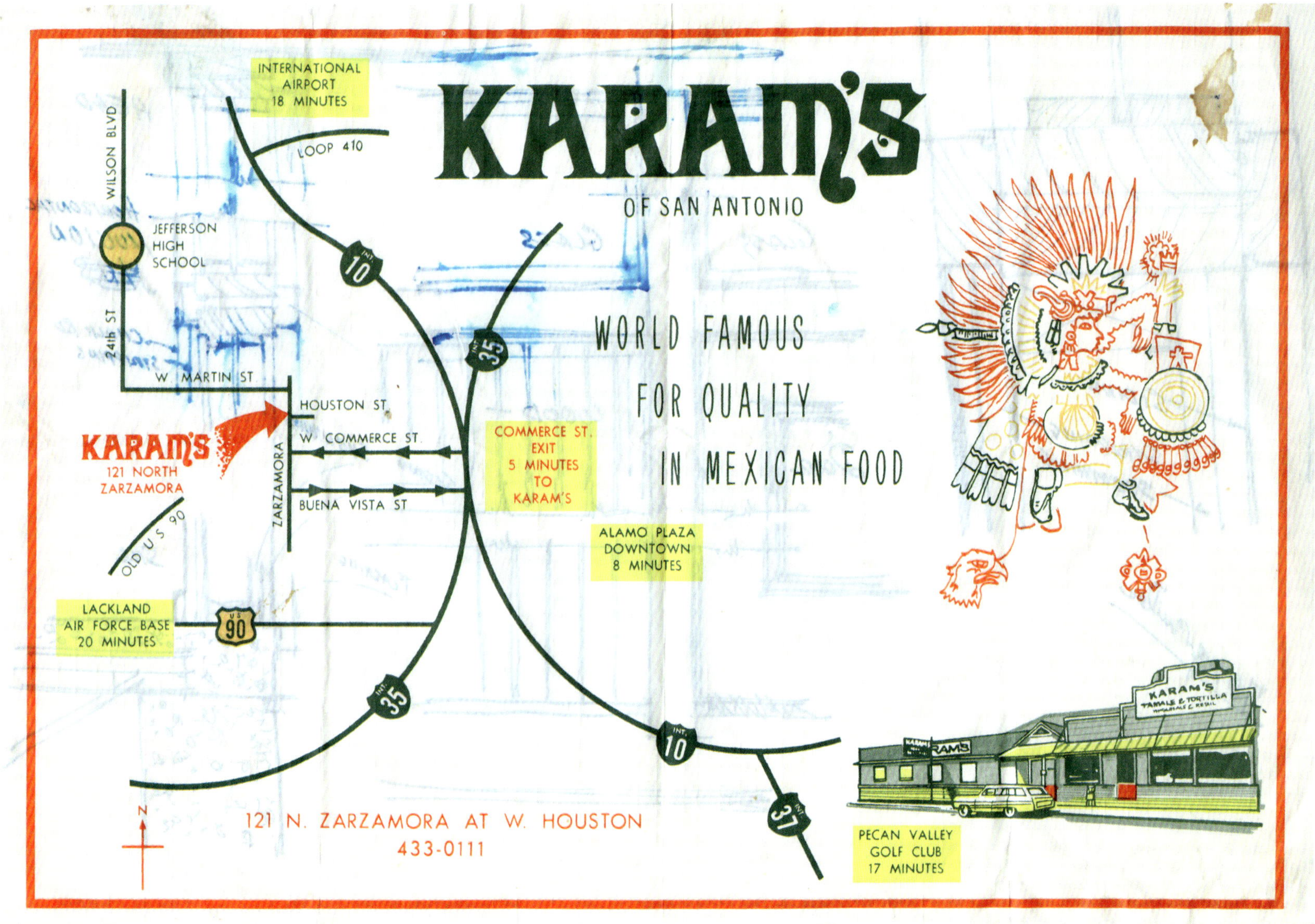

Restaurant placemat, unknown designer, undated

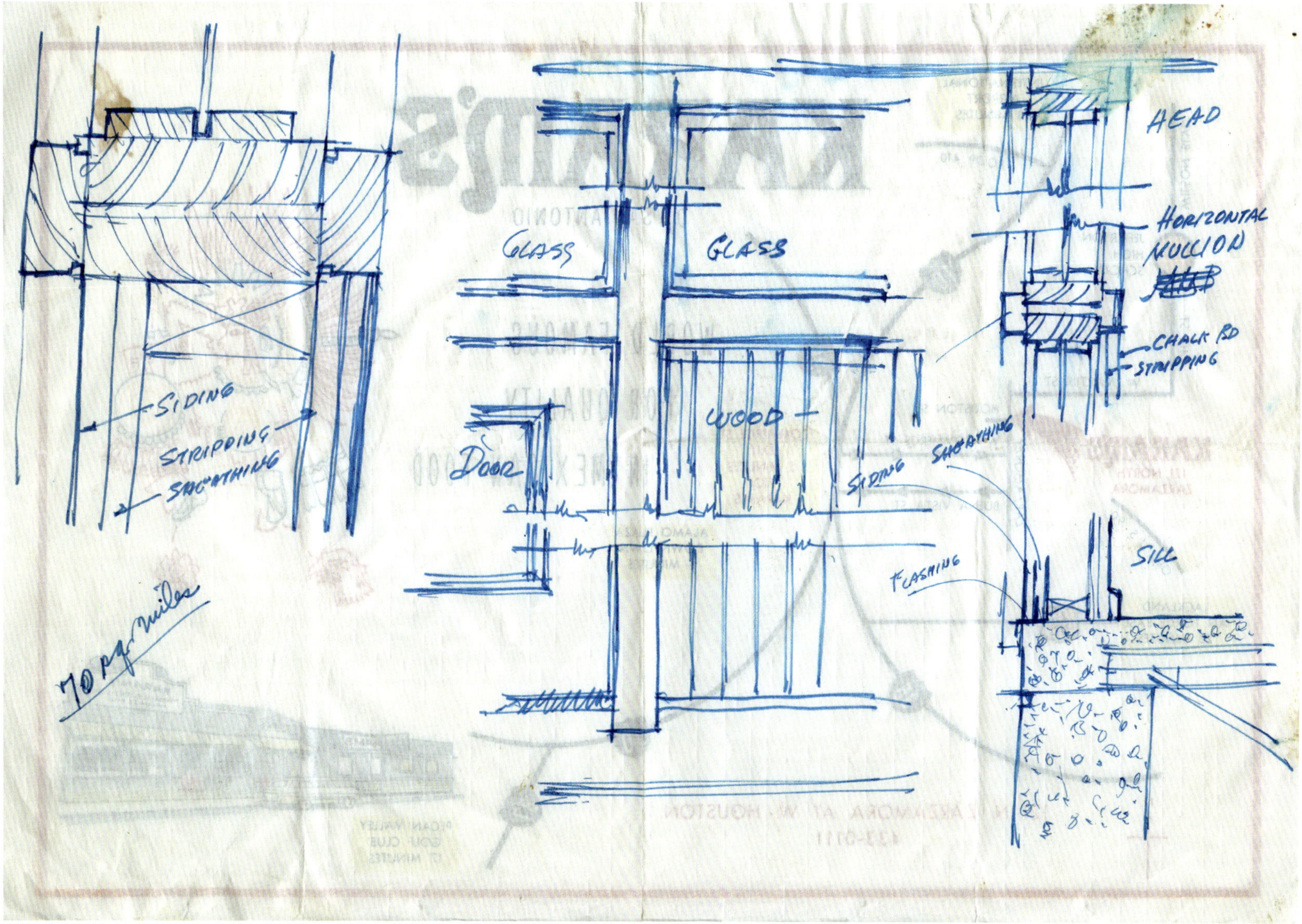

Sketch of glazing detail on verso restaurant placemat, O'Neil Ford, undated

Plans

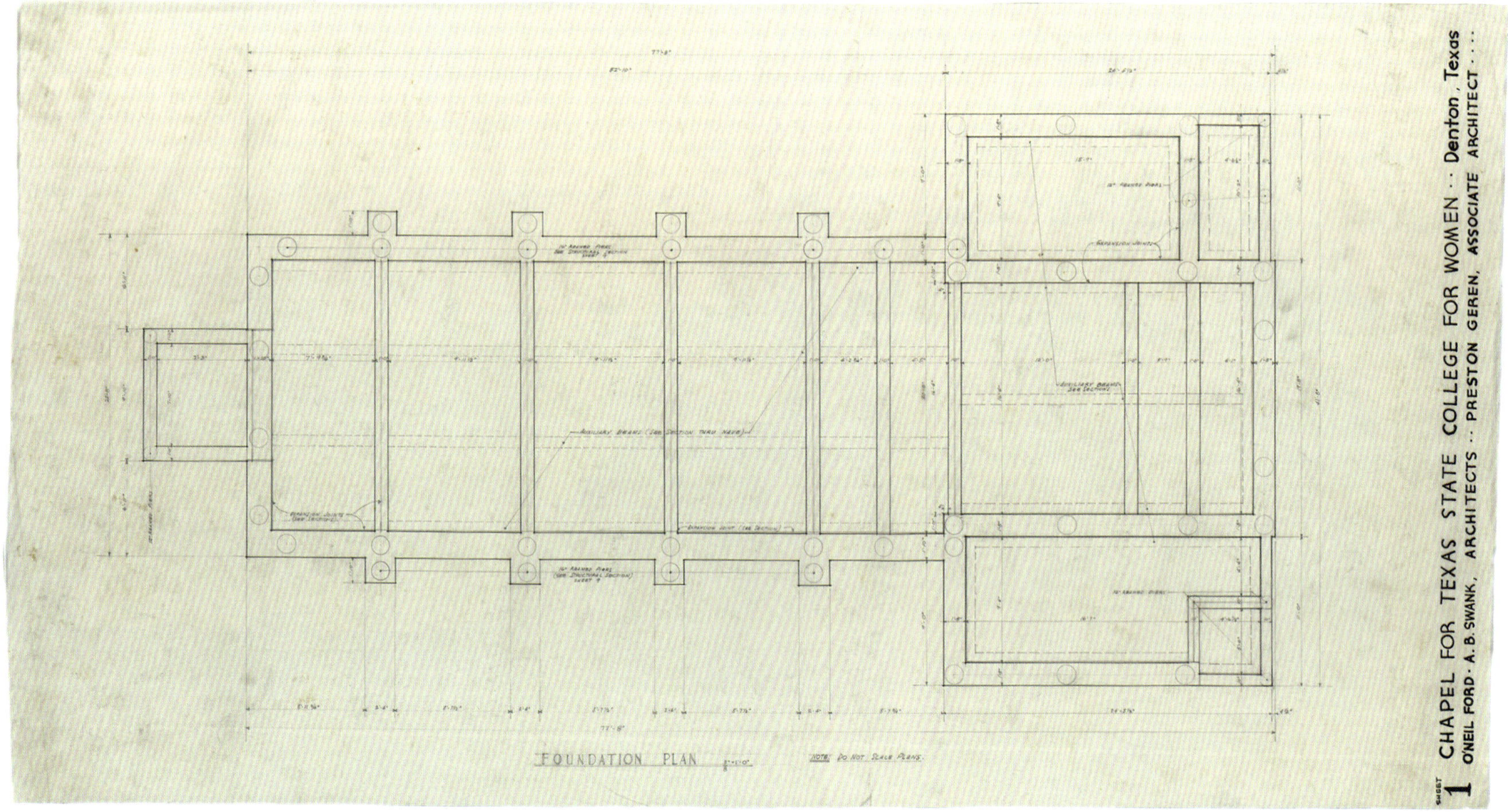

Foundation plan, O'Neil Ford, A.B. Swank, Preston Geren (associate architect)

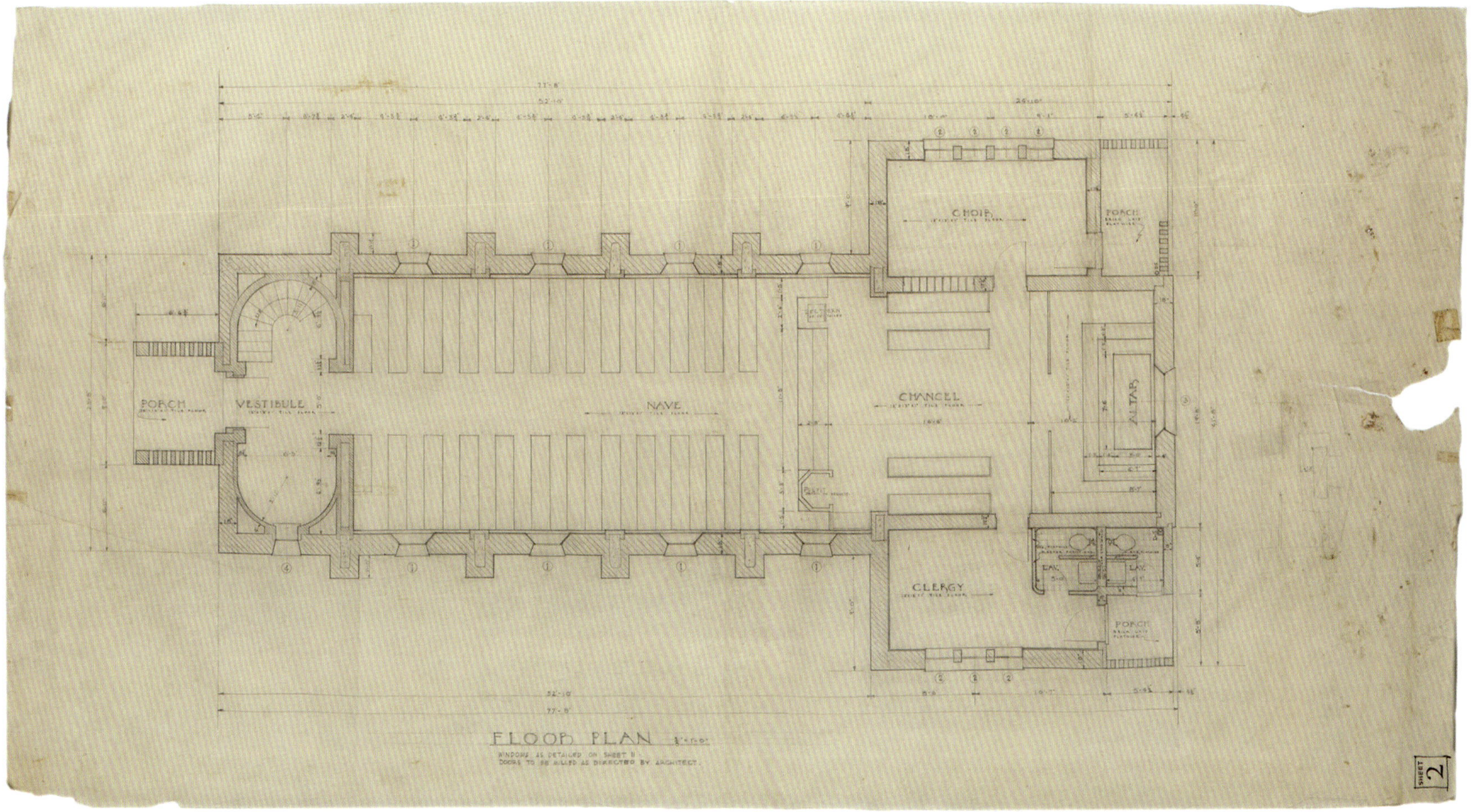

Floor plan, O'Neil Ford, A.B. Swank, Preston Geren (associate architect)

Side elevation, rear elevation, O'Neil Ford, A.B. Swank, Preston Geren (associate architect)

Cross section through nave; front elevation; cornice, window head, rake and soffit; window sill; purlin joint, O'Neil Ford, A.B. Swank, Preston Geren (associate architect)

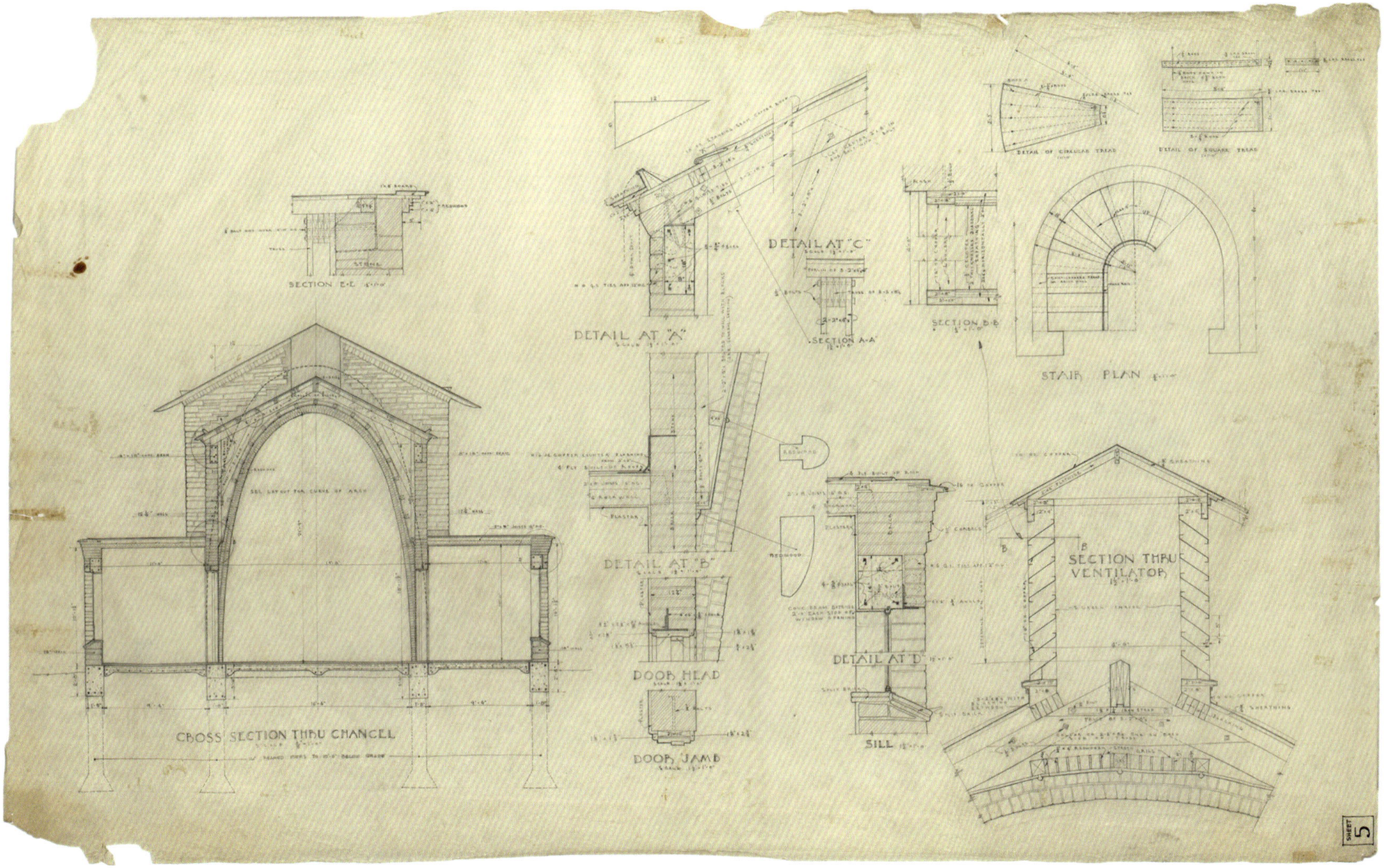

Cross section through chancel; details, stair plan; section through ventilator, O'Neil Ford, A.B. Swank, Preston Geren (associate architect)

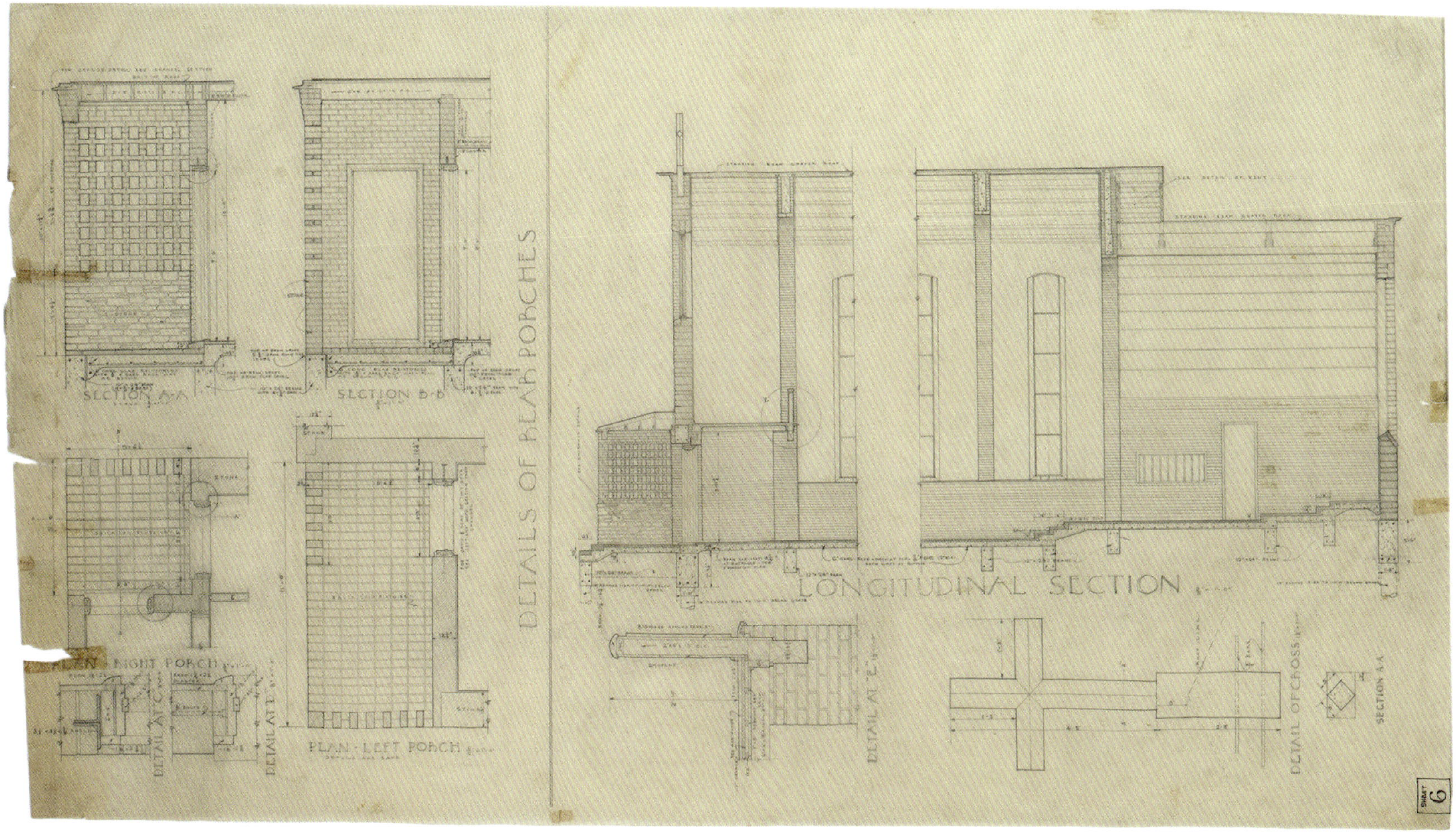

Details of rear porches; longitudinal section and details, O'Neil Ford, A.B. Swank, Preston Geren (associate architect)

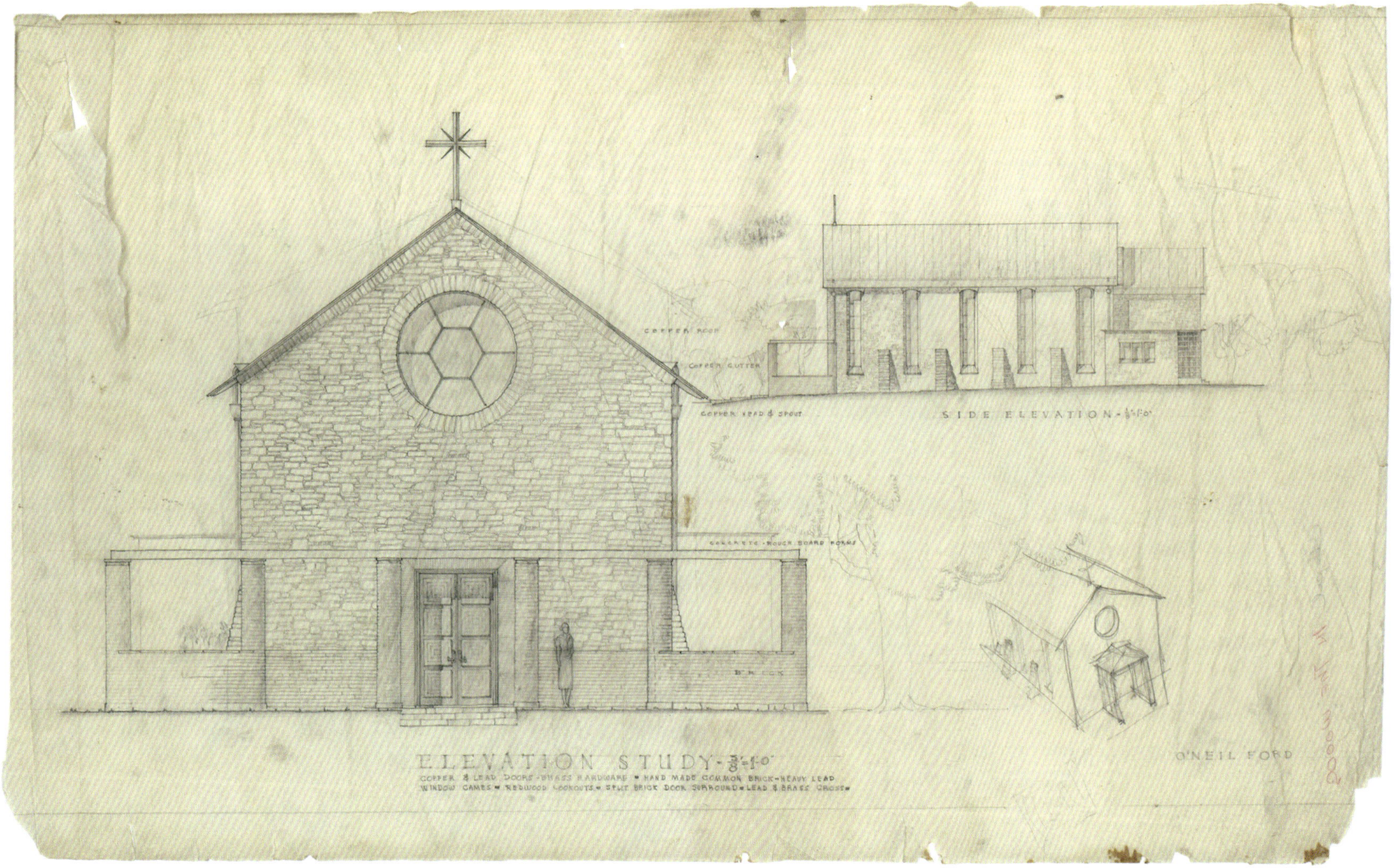

Elevation study, O'Neil Ford, A.B. Swank, Preston Geren (associate architect)

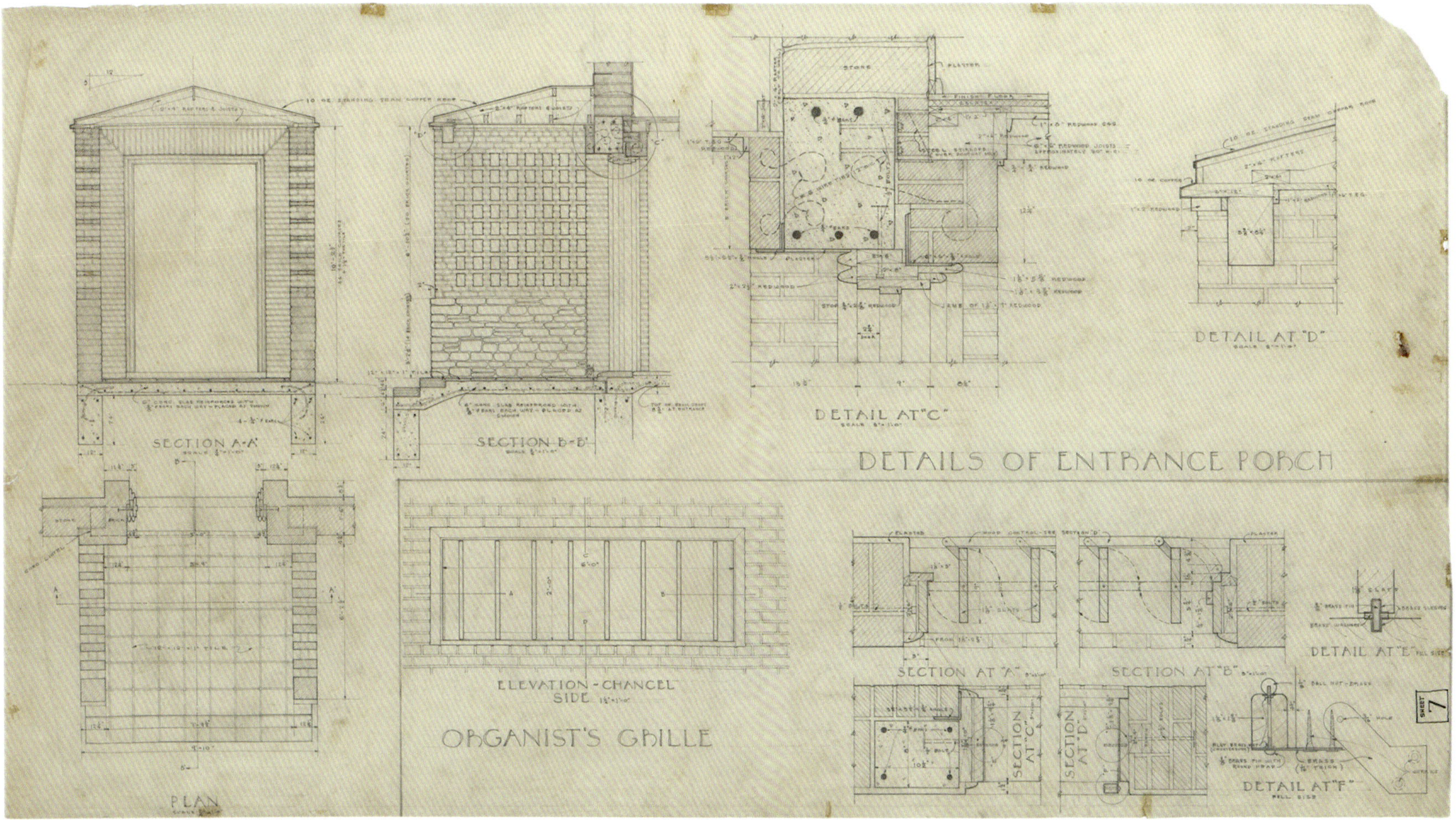

Entrance porch details, sections and plan; organist's grille elevation, sections and details, O'Neil Ford, A.B. Swank, Preston Geren (associate architect)

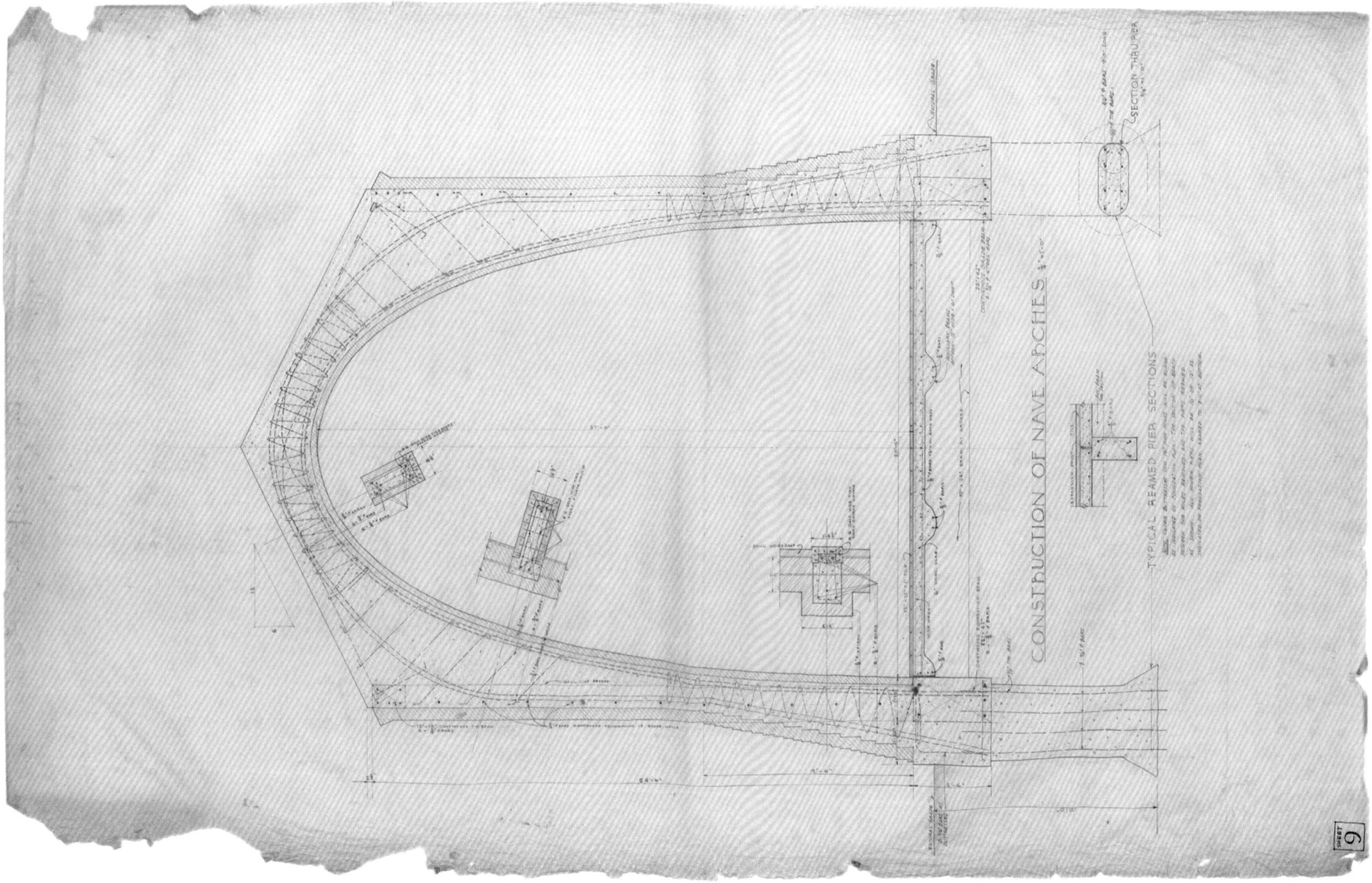

Construction of nave arches, section through pier, typical reamed pier sections and note, O'Neil Ford, A.B. Swank, Preston Geren (associate architect)

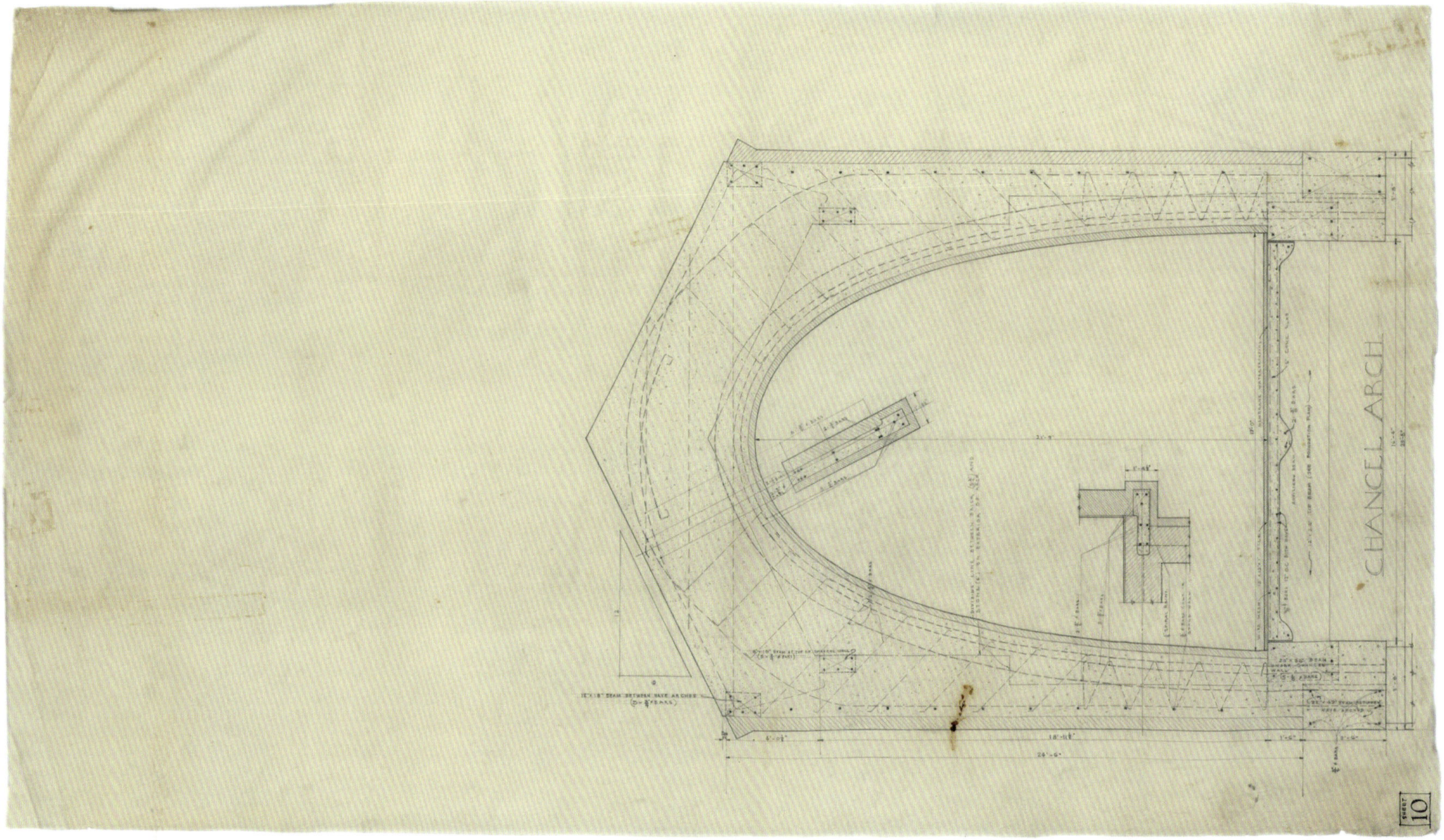

Chancel arch, O'Neil Ford, A.B. Swank, Preston Geren (associate architect)

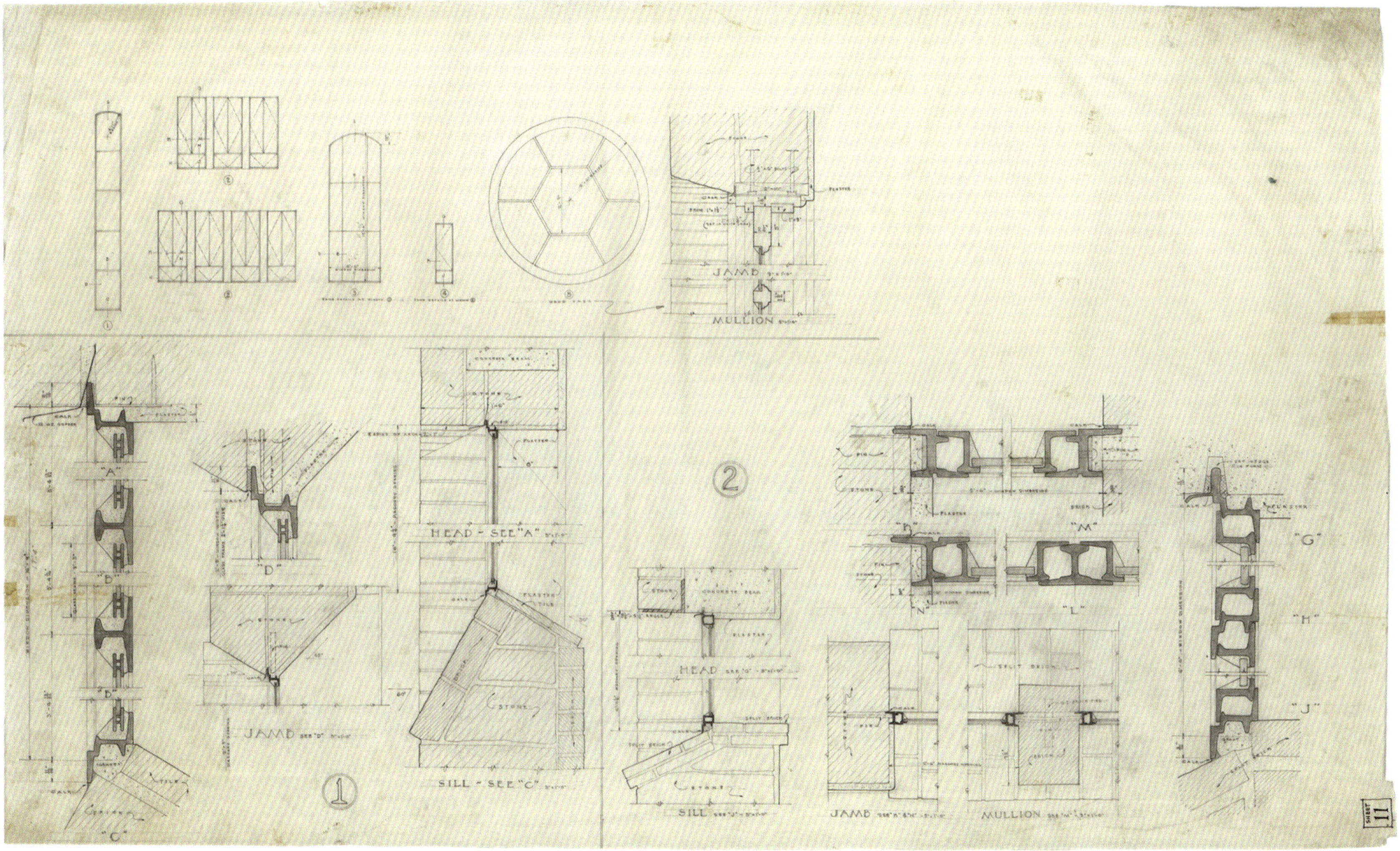

Window types and details of head, sills, jambs and mullions, O'Neil Ford, A.B. Swank, Preston Geren (associate architect)

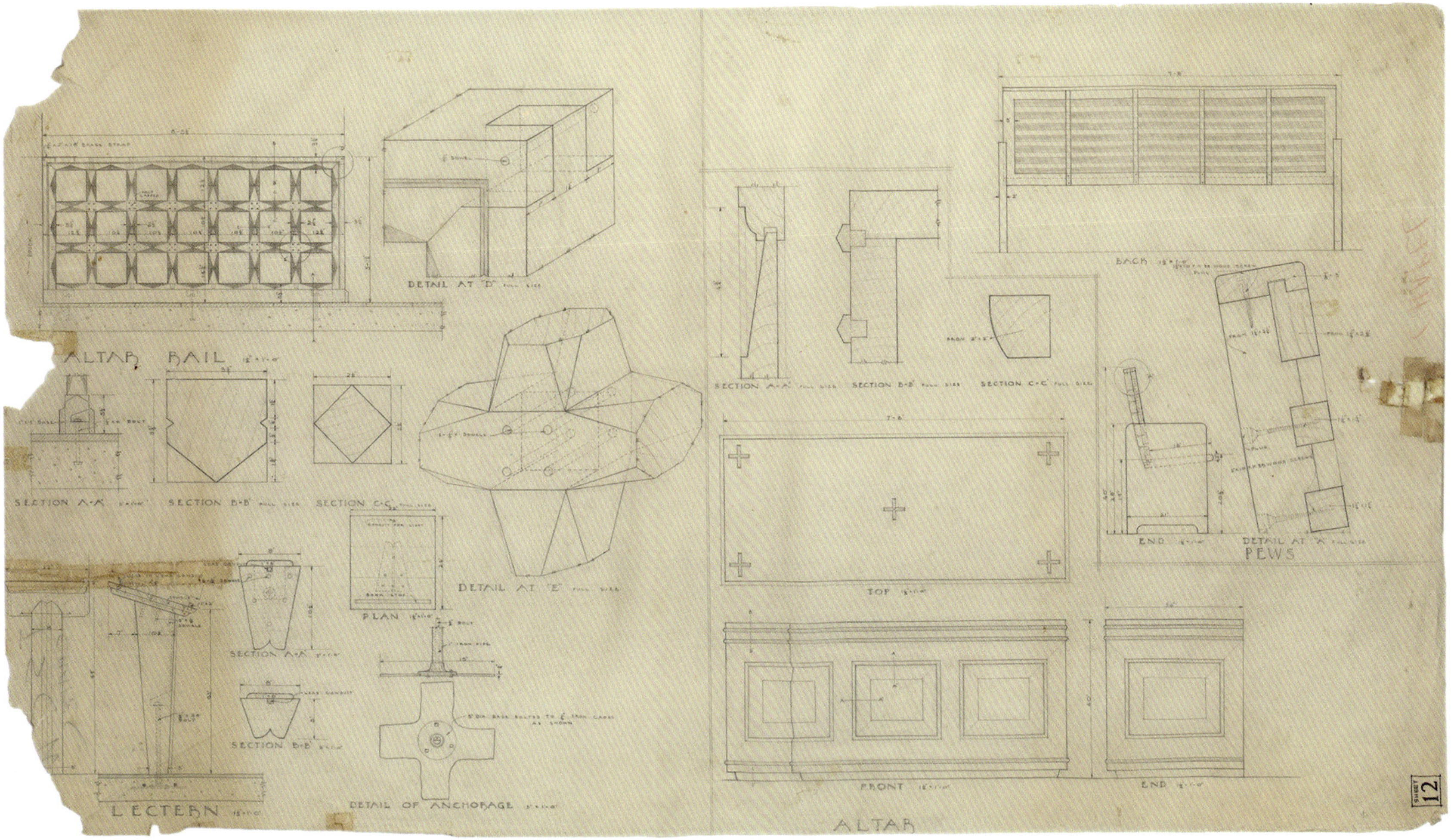

Lectern; altar rail; altar top, front, end sections, pew end and details, O'Neil Ford, A.B. Swank, Preston Geren (associate architect)

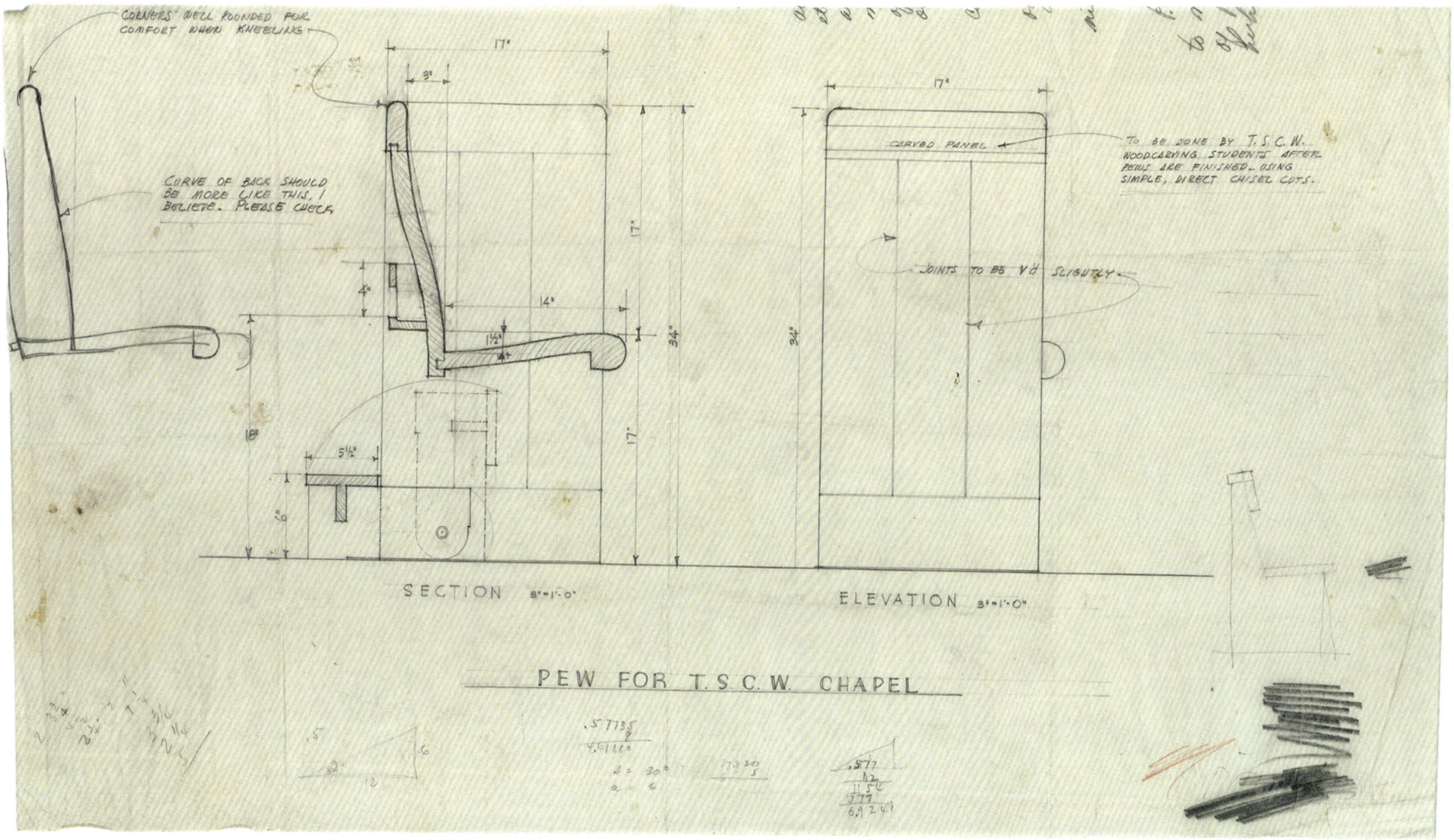

Pew for T.S.C.W. chapel section and elevation, O'Neil Ford, A.B. Swank, Preston Geren (associate architect)

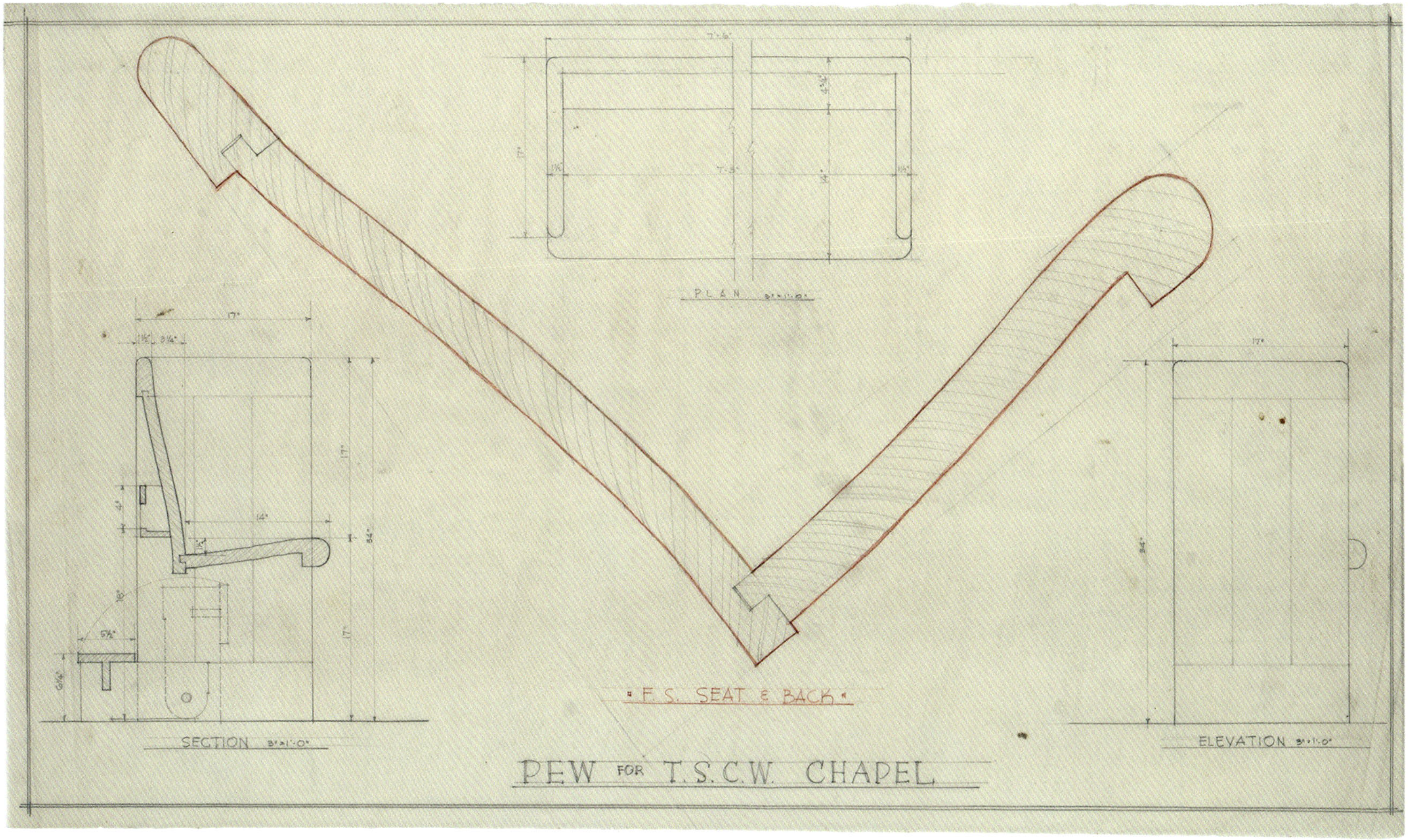

Pew for T.S.C.W. chapel plan, section, elevation full scale seat and back, O'Neil Ford, A.B. Swank, Preston Geren (associate architect)

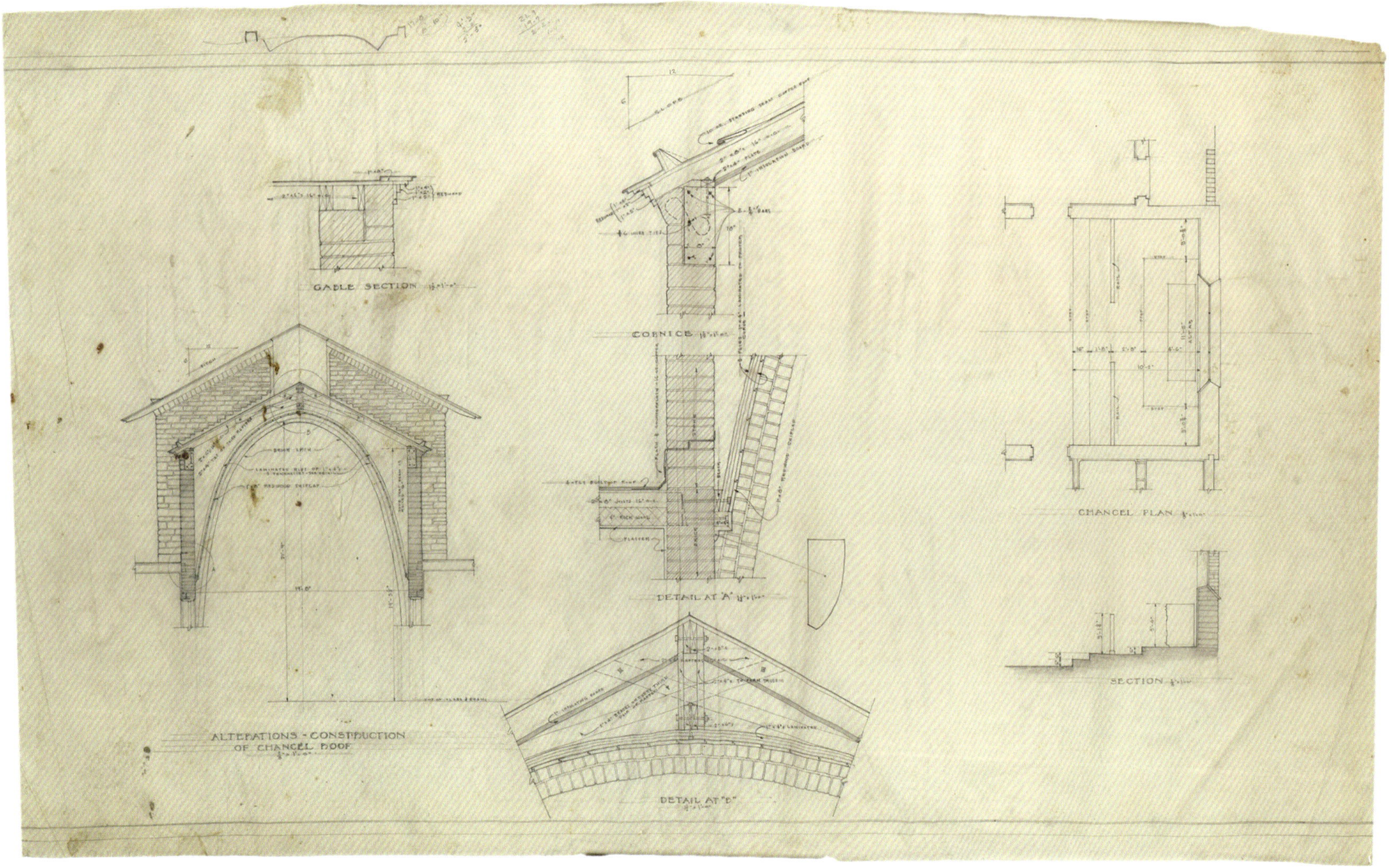

Alterations construction of chapel roof, gable section, details, cornice, chancel plan, section, O'Neil Ford, A.B. Swank, Preston Geren (associate architect)

Bird's eye perspective drawing of exterior of chapel, O'Neil Ford, A.B. Swank, Preston Geren (associate architect)

Period Photographs

Construction of The Little Chapel in the Woods, on the Texas State Women's College campus in Denton, Texas

Construction of The Little Chapel in the Woods, on the Texas State Women's College campus in Denton, Texas

Construction of The Little Chapel in the Woods, on the Texas State Women's College campus in Denton, Texas

Construction of The Little Chapel in the Woods, on the Texas State Women's College campus in Denton, Texas

Construction of The Little Chapel in the Woods, on the Texas State Women's College campus in Denton, Texas

Construction of The Little Chapel in the Woods, on the Texas State Women's College campus in Denton, Texas

Construction of The Little Chapel in the Woods, on the Texas State Women's College campus in Denton, Texas

Construction of the roof of The Little Chapel in the Woods, on the Texas State Women's College campus in Denton, Texas

Construction of the roof of The Little Chapel in the Woods, on the Texas State Women's College campus in Denton, Texas

Construction of the roof of The Little Chapel in the Woods, on the Texas State Women's College campus in Denton, Texas

Construction of The Little Chapel in the Woods, on the Texas State Women's College campus in Denton, Texas, 1939

Construction of The Little Chapel in the Woods, on the Texas State Women's College campus in Denton, Texas, 1939

O'NFM_8

Dedication of The Little Chapel in the Woods, on the Texas State Women's College campus in Denton, Texas.
The photograph shows First Lady Eleanor Roosevelt giving the introduction at the front entrance to the chapel.
November 2, 1939

Front entrance of The Little Chapel in the Woods, Denton, Texas

Front entrance and east side of The Little Chapel in the Woods, on the Texas State Women's College campus in Denton, Texas

Interior of The Little Chapel in the Woods, on the Texas State Women's College campus in Denton, Texas

Interior of The Little Chapel in the Woods, on the Texas State Women's College campus in Denton, Texas

Details of the decorative carvings on the sides of the wooden pews in The Little Chapel in the Woods

Wooden lectern and pulpit with beautifully carved decorations on the brick stage

Large elaborate doors of The Little Chapel in the Woods

Detail of the door handles and decorative carvings on the wooden doors of The Little Chapel in the Woods

Detail shot of the door handles of The Little Chapel in the Woods

Contemporary Photographs

O'NFM_8

LET THEM PRAISE HIS NAME IN THE DANCE
PRAISE YE THE LORD
PSALM 49:3
"O MAY I JOIN THE CHOIR INVISIBLE OF THOSE IMMORTAL DEAD WHO LIVE AGAIN IN MINDS MADE BETTER BY THEIR PRESENCE."
GEORGE ELIOT

NEVER MIND THE
BRICK AND MORTAR
ONLY LET US HAVE
THE LIVING MINDS
TO WORK UPON
MARY LYON
ST. DENIS
ISADORA
LET THEM
PRAISE HIS
NAME IN
THE DANCE
PRAISE
PSALM 49:3

DAMES DE CHARITE
LIFE IS NOT
EASY FOR ANY
OF US BUT:
WHAT OF THAT?
WE MUST HAVE
PERSEVERANCE
AND ABOVE ALL
CONFIDENCE
COST MUST
BE ATTAINED

GLORIA
IN EXCELSIS
DEO

P.150–154 Color Transparencies of the stained glass windows at The Little Chapel in the Woods, Denton, Texas, 1986

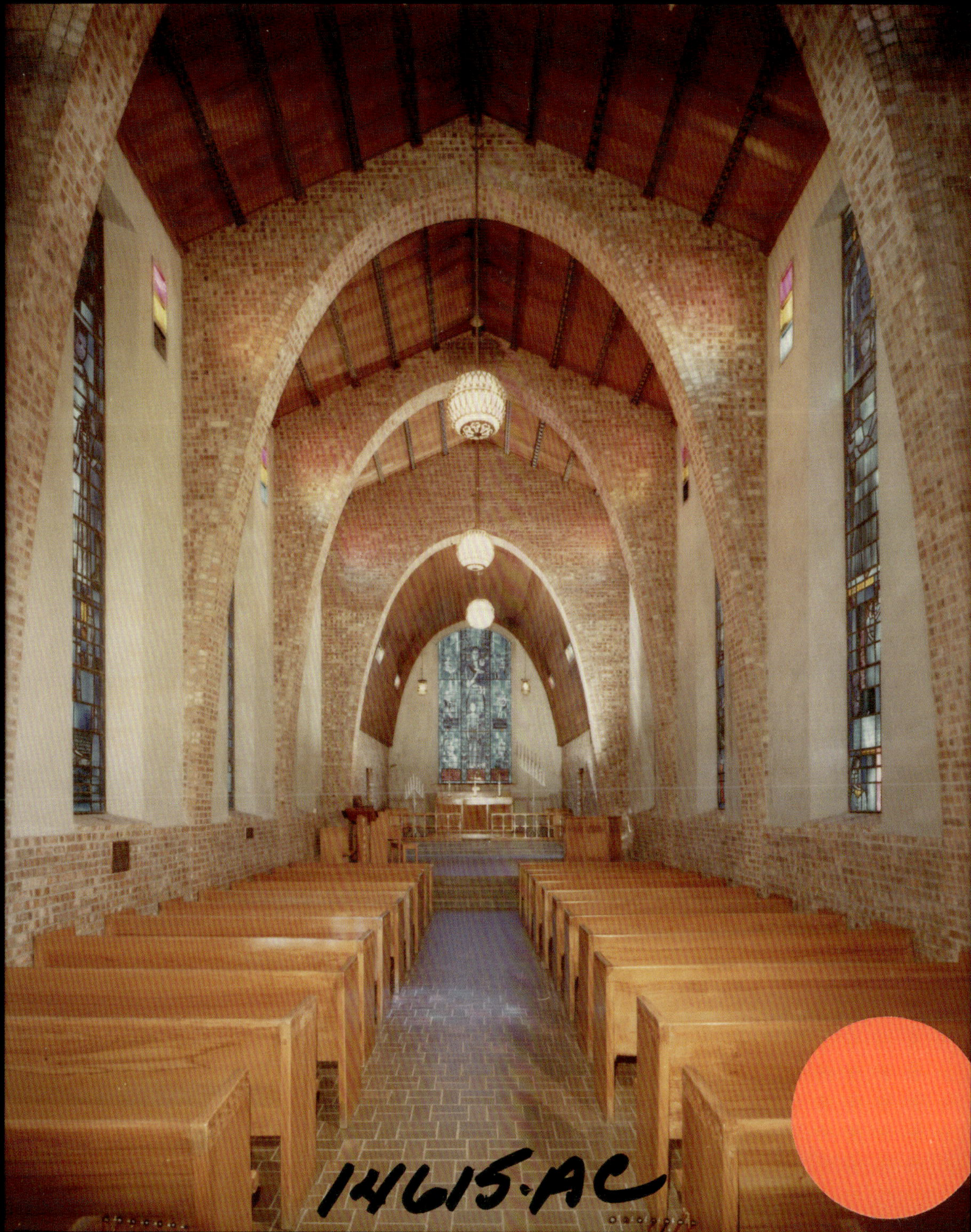

Photograph of the interior of The Little Chapel in the Woods, on the Texas State Women's College campus in Denton, Texas, undated

Beth J. Dodd

Beth Dodd has worked with the University of Texas Libraries architectural collections since 1995, when she was appointed as the first Curator of the Architectural Drawings Collection. During her tenure, she also served as the Head Librarian for the Architecture & Planning Library (2007-2015), administering a branch library in historic Battle Hall, with a distinctive century-old research collection. Her work ranged from establishing the Texas Chapter for the Committee for the Preservation of Architectural Records (COPAR), to evolving services into the digital age. Dodd's efforts with Blake Alexander, through the naming of the archive and establishment of an endowment, secured prominence and funding to support staff expertise and the momentum for innovation. This includes providing opportunities for experiential learning for students at the University's top ranked School of Information studying preservation of the cultural record and archival enterprise.

As Curator of the Alexander Architectural Archives, Dodd continues to direct and manage an innovative full archival program with colleagues and activities that preserves and provides access to archival records. She is a liaison for donors, scholars, and stake-holders in the blended analog & digital scholarship ecosystem, actively supporting collection develop-ment and services related to subject areas taught at the School of Architecture. Prior to her time in Texas, Beth earned her Master of Information and Library Studies at the University of Michigan and worked on cataloging projects at the University of Pittsburgh. At Columbia University's Avery Architectural and Fine Arts Library Department of Drawings and Archives, she cataloged architectural drawings under the Modern Masters processing project.

Brantley Hightower

Brantley Hightower grew up in Arlington, Texas and earned Bachelor of Arts and a Bachelor of Architecture degrees from the University of Texas at Austin. He later earned a Master of Architecture degree from Princeton University. He worked for Perkins & Will in Chicago, Max Levy Architect in Dallas, and Lake|Flato Architects in San Antonio. He founded HiWorks in 2012 and the architecture office's work has since ranged from a community theatre in Fort Stockton to an air traffic control tower in San Antonio. His built work has been widely published and his design work has been recognized in numerous design competitions.

Brantley has taught at the University of Texas at Austin, The University of Texas at Arlington, Texas Tech University, Trinity University, and San Antonio College. His first book, *The Courthouses of Central Texas*, (University of Texas Press, 2015) was published the same year he won the Texas Society of Architects' Young Professional Achievement Honor Award. He is an active contributor to *Texas Architect* magazine and is the host and producer of *The Works* and *The San Antonio Storybook* podcasts. He is a founding board member of San Antonio's Design Forum.

Brantley lives in San Antonio with his wife–who is also an architect–and their two daughters.

Kathryn Holliday

Kathryn Holliday is professor of architecture and founding director of the David Dillon Center for Texas Architecture at the University of Texas at Arlington. She studied architecture, art history, and environmental studies at Williams College and the University of Texas at Austin and she brings this interdisciplinary approach to the classroom and writing. Her most recent project is *The Open-Ended City: David Dillon on Texas Architecture*, a collection of essays by the late architecture critic for the *Dallas Morning News* that delves into issues of downtown redevelopment, urban sprawl, planning, and historic preservation in Texas cities in the age of post-modernism (University of Texas Press, 2019). Her two prior books are *Leopold Eidlitz: Architecture and Idealism in the Gilded Age* (W. W. Norton, 2008), winner of annual book awards from the Victorian Society's New York chapter and the Southeast Chapter of the Society of Architectural Historians, and *Ralph Walker: Architect of the Century* (Rizzoli, 2012). Both monographs argue for an expansion of the canon of American architecture to include controversial figures who pushed to redefine American architecture through arguments for organic and humanist theory. She is at work on *Telephone City: Architecture and Monopoly in the Bell System*, an exploration of technology, design, and telecommunications infrastructure in the United States from the invention of commercial telephone service in 1876 to the breakup of the Bell monopoly in 1984. She is also working longer term to assess the history of urban and suburban development in Dallas-Fort Worth in the 1960s and 1970s, looking especially at the effects of civic fragmentation and urban renewal on the design of democratic space in the Metroplex. Her work has been supported by grants from the National Park Service Civil Rights Grant program, Samuel H. Kress Foundation, Hagley Library, Nasher Foundation, and the McDermott Foundation.

Kathryn E. O'Rourke
Kathryn O'Rourke is associate professor of art history at Trinity University in San Antonio. She is a historian of modern architecture whose interests include many subjects in Latin America, the United States, and Europe. She received her B.A. in Architecture from Wellesley College and her M.A. and Ph.D. in the History of Art from the University of Pennsylvania.

O'Rourke is the author of *Modern Architecture in Mexico City: History, Representation, and the Shaping of a Capital* (University of Pittsburgh Press, 2016), which received the Alice Davis Hitchcock Book Award from the Society of Architectural Historians, and is the editor of *O'Neil Ford on Architecture* (University of Texas Press in 2019), a finalist for the Ramirez Family Award for Most Significant Scholarly Book from the Texas Institute of Letters. She has also published essays on Mexican architectural rationalism and public health care reform, Ludwig Mies van der Rohe's work in Latin America, the art of Diego Rivera, and landscape architecture in Mexico City. She is currently at work on a book manuscript, *Archaism and Humanism in Modern Architecture.*

Katie Pierce Meyer
Katie Pierce Meyer is a librarian, archivist and architectural historian. She is the Head of Architectural Collections at the University of Texas at Austin. Pierce Meyer received her B.A. in Philosophy from Southwestern University and her M.A.in Architectural History and M.S. and PhD in Information Studies from the University of Texas at Austin. Prior to accepting her current position at the University of Texas Libraries, she has held positions as Humanities Librarian for Architecture and Planning and project manager for the Charles W. Moore Archives at the Alexander Architectural Archives.

Pierce Meyer's research focuses on the co-construction of the built environment and the preservation of architectural artifacts as traces of socio-technical networks. She has published on technology and artifacts in architectural practice, preserving born-digital architectural records, archival education, and faculty perceptions on library collections.

Nancy Sparrow
Nancy Sparrow, Curatorial Assistant for Public Services at the Alexander Architectural Archives, has been working with architectural collections at the University of Texas at Austin since 1989. Prior to her current work with the public, Nancy processed collections leading to the creation of the Alexander's first archival finding aids under a Title II-C grant from the United States Department of Education.

Nancy has conducted thousands of research appointments, including in-depth reference consultations, instruction sessions, orientations, curated tours and open houses. In this capacity, she is the Alexander's liaison with the University's School of Architecture faculty, staff and students; the UT community; citizens of Texas; and scholars from around the world, building relationships that result in scholarly output and collection development.

Nancy oversees digitization orders from property owners, architects working on projects, students, faculty and scholar's working on publications which often requires copyright guidance. This work includes both cataloging and publishing files into the University of Texas Libraries Collections Portal. For exhibitions, Nancy serves as both registrar for national and international exhibition loans as well as curator for exhibitions held in the historic Battle Hall reading room. Her work includes the centennial show for Battle Hall and many others assisting student curators. Nancy initiated and developed the *To Better Know a Building* exhibition series, inaugurated in 2014 with the Kimbell Art Museum, and has continued featuring other prominent works including The Little Chapel, Charles Moore's Orinda House, the School of Architecture's Solar Decathlon NexusHaus, and the University of Texas Tower. This series has offered opportunities for collaboration including additional feature publications such as this monograph.

Wilfried Wang
O´Neil Ford Centennial Professor in Architecture at the University of Texas at Austin. Together with Barbara Hoidn, he is founder of the office of Hoidn Wang Partner, Berlin. Wang studied architecture in London, where he was in partnership with John Southall. In 1979 he was founding co-editor of *9H* Magazine and co-director of the 9H Gallery from 1985 to 1990. From 1995 to 2000 he was director of the German Architecture Museum. He has taught at the Polytechnic of North London, University College London, ETH Zurich, Harvard University, and University of Navarra. Wang is the author of various architectural publications. He is a foreign member of the Royal Swedish Academy of Arts; a member of The Academy of Arts, Berlin; and an honorary member of the Portuguese Chamber of Architects. He received an honorary doctorate from the Royal Institute of Technology, Stockholm.

Photo and Drawing Credits

Cover Mark Phillips, photographer
3 Frank D. Welch collection, Alexander Architectural Archives, University of Texas Libraries, The University of Texas at Austin
4 ArkDes Collections ARKM.1973-05-08769
5 ARKM.1973-103-084-021
6 Historisches Archiv des Erzbistums Köln bzw. AEK, Nachlass Rudolf und Maria Schwarz
7 Bildarchiv Monheim Baukunst, #16855, Krefeld, (2019)
8 Peter Celsing Archive, Stockholm
9 archipicture.eu
10 Dimitri Pikionis Archive, Neohellenic Architecture Archives, Benaki Museum, Athens, Greece
12 O'Neil Ford collection; Leslie Gill, Contact Sheet of O'Neil Ford, ca. 1948, photograph, Copyright © by the Estate of Leslie Gill
14 – 26 O'Neil Ford collection
28 Photo courtesy of Cliff Knight
30 O'Neil Ford collection; National Youth Administration photographs
31 O'Neil Ford collection; Rick Gardener, photographer, Information for copyright permission: Unable to locate any information
32 O'Neil Ford collection
33 O'Neil Ford collection; Jeremiah Bragstad, photographer, Information for copyright permission: Unable to locate any information
34 O'Neil Ford collection
35 Brantley Hightower
37 O'Neil Ford collection
38 Brantley Hightower
39 O'Neil Ford collection
40 – 45 Image Courtesy of the TWU Libraries Woman's Collection, Texas Woman's University, Denton
48 Denton Public Library
50 (L) Archives of Texas Woman's University, UAP 18.02.01
(R) Archives of Texas Woman's University, UAP 18.02.35
51 Denton Public Library
53 Sabetheus (Jim Mills), GNU Free Documentation License; Creative Commons License Attribution-Share Alike
55 (L) Archives of Texas Woman's University, UAP 18.02.13
(R) Archives of Texas Woman's University, UAP 18.02.36
56 (L) Archives of Texas Woman's University
(M) Kathryn E. O'Rourke
(R) Kathryn E. O'Rourke
58 (L) Kathryn E. O'Rourke
(M) Archives of Texas Woman's University
(R) Kathryn E. O'Rourke
59 (L) Archives of Texas Woman's University
(M) Archives of Texas Woman's University
(R) Kathryn E. O'Rourke
61 – 62 Kathryn E. O'Rourke
63 (L) Kathryn E. O'Rourke
(R) Bonnie Tipton Wilson
64 2010 Artists Rights Society (ARS), © 2020 Banco de México Diego Rivera Frida Kahlo Museums Trust, Mexico, D.F. / Artists Rights Society (ARS), New York
65 Image in the Public Domain
66 Harvard Art Museums/Busch-Reisinger Museum, Gift of Walter Gropius, Photo: © President and Fellows of Harvard College, Accession Number: BRGA.8.5, © The Josef and Anni Albers Foundation / Artists Rights Society (ARS), New York, [2020]
67 Kathryn E. O'Rourke. 2010 Artists Rights Society (ARS) [RIVERA rights]
68 Kathryn E. O'Rourke
74 – 117 O'Neil Ford collection
118 – 121 O'Neil Ford collection; National Youth Administration photographs
122 O'Neil Ford collection; Rick Gardener, photographer, Information for copyright permission: Unable to locate any information
123 Denton Public Library
124 O'Neil Ford collection National Youth Administration photographs
125 (L) O'Neil Ford collection
(R) Denton Public Library
127 – 131 Denton Public Library
134 – 149 Mark Phillips
150 – 154 Eugene George collection, Alexander Architectural Archives, University of Texas Libraries, The University of Texas at Austin
155 O'Neil Ford collection; Rick Gardener, photographer, Information for copyright permission: Unable to locate any information
156 Mark Phillips